Enriching Primary English

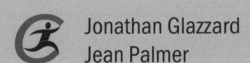

Jonathan Glazzard
Jean Palmer

CRITICAL TEACHING

British Library Cataloguing in Publication Data
A CIP record for this book is available from the British Library

ISBN: 978-1-909682-49-8

This book is also available in the following e-book formats:

MOBI ISBN: 978-1-909682-50-4
EPUB ISBN: 978-1-909682-51-1
Adobe e-reader ISBN: 978-1-909682-52-8

Cover and text design by Greensplash Limited
Project Management by Out of House Publishing
Printed and bound in Great Britain by Bell & Bain, Glasgow

Most of our titles are available in a range of electronic formats. To order please go to our website www.criticalpublishing.com or contact our distributor, NBN International, 10 Thornbury Road, Plymouth PL6 7PP, telephone 01752 202301 or email orders@nbninternational.com.

Critical Publishing
152 Chester Road
Northwich
CW8 4AL
www.criticalpublishing.com

MIX
Paper from
responsible sources
FSC® C007785

Contents

Meet the authors

Jonathan Glazzard has been teaching since 1995. He has worked across the early years, Key Stage 1 and Key Stage 2 as a primary school teacher, special educational needs co-ordinator and assistant headteacher. Since 2005 he has worked at the University of Huddersfield, where he is a senior lecturer and University Teaching Fellow. He teaches on the primary English modules and is course leader for the BA and PGCE Primary Education courses and the MA in Early Childhood Studies. Jonathan is responsible for leading the primary initial teacher training provision. He is passionate about promoting creative approaches to teaching which inspire practitioners and children.

Jean Palmer joined the University of Huddersfield in January 2013 and is a Senior Lecturer on the BA Early Primary course and the PGCE Primary course, where she is also partnership and placements co-ordinator and is a tutor for English, history, geography and PSED. Jean has worked in Kirklees schools since 1996 and has over 30 years' experience of working with teachers and young people. Over the past 16 years she has worked in primary schools as a teacher, subject leader, Advanced Skills Teacher (English), governor and LA officer. She has taught across the primary phases and acted as senior mentor for GTP students. She was the lead consultant in Kirklees for the Every Child a Reader programme and is an accredited trainer for the Reading Recovery programme.

Introduction

The *Progress in International Reading Literacy Study* (PIRLS, 2011) compares the attainment and attitudes in reading of over 200,000 nine- and ten-year-olds around the world. The study is repeated every five years and the next study will take place in 2016. In 2011, the top-performing countries in reading were Hong Kong, the Russian Federation, Finland and Singapore. Although England demonstrated an improvement in overall reading achievement from 2006–11, it is not listed as one of the top-performing countries. Additionally, the study identified that the gap between boys' and girls' achievement was greater in England than in most other countries. Girls performed better than boys in reading in England and in most other countries (PIRLS, 2011). The study found that the pupils who enjoyed reading also attained higher scores. However, despite the fact that 20 per cent of pupils in England reported that they did not enjoy reading, England performed well above the international average and the best readers in England were among the best in the world. However, this rosy picture masks the fact that England had a greater proportion of weaker readers than many higher-performing countries (PIRLS, 2011).

Worldwide, high achievement in reading was associated with children from more affluent socio-economic backgrounds, and students from economically disadvantaged backgrounds demonstrated the lowest levels of achievement (PIRLS, 2011). A supportive home environment and an early start to reading are crucial in shaping children's development in reading (PIRLS, 2011). Students with positive attitudes to reading demonstrated higher levels of achievement than those with negative attitudes, and children with greater self-efficacy or high self-esteem about themselves as readers are typically better readers (PIRLS, 2011). Successful schools had better access to resources such as books, and achievement was lower in schools that had more limited resources.

Becoming a good reader is too important to be left to chance. We argue that all children have an entitlement to high-quality teaching and access to resources and support to enable them to read well, regardless of their socio-economic circumstances, gender, ethnicity, the school they attend and the country in which they live. Reading unlocks the door to a wide range of opportunities which are denied to those who are unable to read and comprehend. The long tail of underachievement in reading (Tymms and Merrell, 2010) in England and other countries, including the United States, New Zealand, Scotland and Singapore, is completely unacceptable and must be addressed by governments immediately. It is our belief that all children can learn to read.

Although this book focuses on spoken language, reading and writing, addressing the long tail of underachievement in reading will go a long way to addressing underachievement in other areas of the curriculum. Children who read more demonstrate higher levels of achievement than those who read less. Avid readers develop a broad and rich vocabulary, which will improve the quality of their written expression. Through reading they absorb the rules about grammar and punctuation, which supports them to produce more sophisticated writing. However, the development of children's spoken language and auditory skills needs to be prioritised above reading and writing because spoken language underpins development in reading and writing. Children who are unable to think and communicate in sentences will find it more difficult to write in sentences. Without linguistic comprehension, pupils will be unable to understand the words they read, and a restricted vocabulary will restrict the quality of their writing. Children will find the task of reading more difficult if they are unable to listen to the sounds of the phonemes they are trying to blend to make words. To improve overall achievement in literacy, teachers need to prioritise speaking and listening by creating spaces for communication. Understanding the inter-relationship between speaking and listening, reading and writing is so important because it helps teachers to understand why children may be underachieving in English.

Ofsted (2012) highlighted that 40 per cent of children were not secure in the full range of English skills by the time they started Year 1. Scores for writing remain the weakest of all areas of assessment in the Early Years Foundation Stage (EYFS). Girls achieve better than boys in English at the age of five and the achievement gap is wider in writing (Ofsted, 2012). Ofsted (2012) also notes that standards in English in Key Stage 1 did not improve in the period from 2008 to 2011, and a sizeable minority of pupils were not secure in the basic skills of literacy before they moved into Key Stage 2. In Key Stage 2, attainment in English remained static from 2008 to 2011 and an insufficient number of pupils demonstrated achievement at the highest levels, with a fifth of pupils failing to reach national expectations (Ofsted, 2012). Too much teaching of English requires improvement and schools did not always demonstrate a systematic approach to developing pupils' early communication skills (Ofsted, 2012).

Given this depressing context, it is not surprising that the government has set the bar high in the new national curriculum (DfE, 2013). The curriculum sets out exacting expectations for every year group in order to drive forward standards in English. There is greater focus on grammar and reading for enjoyment and the use of correct registers of communication. We support these changes and believe that they will help to raise attainment in English. The challenging expectations place an onus on providers of teacher training and continuing professional development to ensure that both current and future teachers have the knowledge and skills required to implement the new curriculum. Teacher educators need to ensure that the quality of initial teacher training is high so that all trainees have the knowledge and skills needed to teach the full breadth of content from Year 1 to Year 6. At the same time as ensuring that trainees have good subject knowledge per se, teacher educators also must make sure that trainees have a secure knowledge of the pedagogical approaches needed to make their lessons interesting and exciting. We believe that outstanding teachers are able to develop lessons which engage, motivate and excite children. We also believe that the very best teachers are capable of igniting children's enthusiasm to the point where children are obsessed about what they are learning. In this book, we focus on supporting you to develop a pedagogical toolkit that will not only enthuse you, but will also get your pupils obsessed about English. The best teacher will be able to get children obsessed about subordinate clauses or fronted adverbials. It is not about the *what* of teaching; it is about the *how*. The national curriculum tells you what to teach but it does not tell you how. You can read other texts to support your subject knowledge. This is a book which essentially focuses on pedagogy and enrichment strategies.

We hope this book achieves the intended purpose, which is to encourage you to be passionate about teaching English. We hope it inspires you and, in turn, we hope that you inspire, engage, enthuse and motivate your pupils.

References

Department for Education (DfE) (2013) *The National Curriculum in England: Key Stages 1 and 2 Framework Document*. London: DfE.

Office for Standards in Education (Ofsted) (2012) *Moving English Forward: Action to Raise Standards in English*. London: Ofsted.

PIRLS (2011) *International Results in Reading: Executive Summary*. Boston: TIMSS and PIRLS International Study Center.

Tymms, P, and Merrell, C (2010) Standards and Quality in English Primary Schools over time, in Alexander, R (ed) *The Cambridge Primary Review Research Surveys*. Abingdon: Routledge, pp 435–60.

1 Spoken language: Key Stage 1

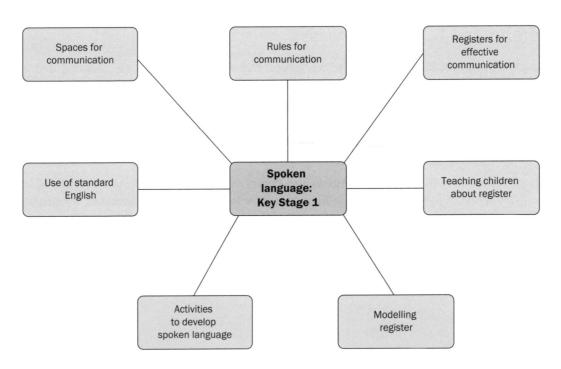

Teachers' Standards

TS3: Demonstrate good subject and curriculum knowledge

Trainees must:

*   have a secure knowledge of the relevant subject(s) and curriculum areas, foster and maintain pupils' interest in the subject, and address misunderstandings;

*   demonstrate a critical understanding of developments in the subject and curriculum

areas, and promote the value of scholarship;

* demonstrate an understanding of and take responsibility for promoting high standards of literacy, articulacy and the correct use of standard English, whatever the teacher's specialist subject.

National curriculum links

Spoken language

The national curriculum highlights the importance of developing spoken language across the whole curriculum. It emphasises that spoken language underpins the development of reading and writing and therefore pupils should have opportunities to develop competence in both their spoken language and their listening skills. The statutory overarching requirements for all year groups state that pupils must have opportunities to: listen and respond; ask questions; build their vocabulary and participate in a range of activities including collaborative conversations, discussions, presentations, debates and role play. The national curriculum also emphasises the need to teach pupils about different *registers* for effective communication.

Introduction

Spoken language and the development of children's listening skills should be embedded throughout the subjects of the national curriculum as a tool for promoting learning. Their use is not just limited to English and you should plan for pupils to use spoken language in a range of different contexts and for different purposes. You cannot assume that children will start their primary education with accurate spoken language and good listening skills. Even if these skills are secure, they may not know how spoken language should be adjusted to take into account the audience and the social setting. You may hear children and parents speaking to each other in inappropriate ways and children may continue to use casual forms of communication with teachers and other adults in school if parents have not explicitly told them that the way they communicate with adults must differ from the way they communicate with each other. If teachers fail to address this issue, children will enter the adult world without adequate knowledge of the fact that communication must be adjusted to take into account the audience, topic of conversation, purpose and location.

Good spoken language provides the foundations for writing development. Children who cannot speak in sentences will find it difficult to write in sentences. Listening and attention is a prerequisite for subsequent reading development. Children who are unable to tune in to sounds will find it difficult to distinguish between different phonemes and this will hinder the process of decoding. Developing good spoken language and being a good listener are essential for subsequent success in the adult world. Effective communication is a necessary requirement of most jobs and essential for dealing with social encounters in both formal and informal settings. Children born into socially deprived environments may start school with under-developed language and communication skills and it is critical that early intervention and support is provided to improve this aspect of development.

Spaces for communication

According to Ofsted in their report *Moving English Forward: Action to Raise Standards in English* (Ofsted, 2012):

> *Previous subject inspections have identified a lack of emphasis on explicit, planned teaching of speaking and listening. This remains the case. Speaking is more commonly seen in schools as a way of supporting writing. Practice in this area has been resistant to change for many years. One reason is that teachers understandably prioritise pupils' work in reading and writing because they feature more prominently in national tests and examinations. What this report wishes to emphasise is the importance of developing pupils' speaking and listening in the early years that children are in school.*
>
> (Ofsted, 2012, p 48)

Key findings in this Ofsted report are listed below.

- Teachers tend not to identify objectives for speaking and listening as priorities for learning.

- Speaking and listening tended to happen incidentally rather than being explicitly taught.

- Although there were role-play areas in early years classrooms, inspectors were surprised that staff spent little time supporting children's play by engaging them in conversations.

- In the most effective settings, staff worked hard to promote spoken language and vocabulary development.

- In the most effective settings, staff saw vocabulary development as central to their work, particularly in early years settings.

- The best schools had adopted a systematic approach to teaching speaking and listening in which the skills taught in one year were progressively extended in the subsequent year.

- Teachers need to explicitly teach speaking and listening.

(Ofsted, 2012)

Developing spaces for communication is fundamental to establishing a learning environment in which spoken language plays a fundamental part in promoting learning. Children in early years settings need rich play-based learning opportunities. Teachers and other adults need to interact with children in these spaces using dialogue which promotes thinking. Through skilled questioning, practitioners can advance children's cognitive development. Carefully selected use of vocabulary by adults during these interactions will extend children's vocabulary. Children need planned opportunities to learn through collaborative conversations, discussions, debates and presentations and some of these strategies will be discussed later in this chapter.

Research suggests that children's ability to communicate on entry to school has declined in recent years (Communication Trust, 2010). Children are starting school with lower levels of spoken language and vocabulary than they had 30 years ago, and there is evidence to suggest that some children now start school without even knowing their own name (Communication Trust, 2010). Within this context, it is absolutely critical that teachers are skilled and knowledgeable in this aspect of the curriculum and understand how to enable children to make progress. Limited vocabulary development will have a detrimental impact on reading development, and lack of spoken language will have a detrimental impact on writing development. Immersing children into a rich language context will have a profound positive impact on their understanding and use of language and their vocabulary will improve. Planning opportunities for children to collaborate and use talk throughout the curriculum will be an essential step to aid children's development. Adults who provide correct models of spoken English and introduce pupils to a wide and rich vocabulary will have a significant positive impact on children's development. Valuing spoken language as an output for learning is critical to improving provision. As a trainee teacher, you need to value children talking about learning and you need to explicitly plan for outputs which focus solely on children's spoken language. Focusing on spoken language and vocabulary development as a way of improving children's communication is essential in order to develop children as speakers, readers and writers.

Registers for effective communication

The ability to alter spoken language according to audience, topic, purpose and location is known as *register*. The way we speak to others fundamentally depends on:

* *who* we are speaking to;
* *what* is being talked about;
* *why* the conversation is taking place;
* *where* the conversation is taking place.

Most adults know that it is important to select and use *appropriate registers* for effective communication. To illustrate this, think about the way you converse with your friends during a social occasion. You probably would not converse in the same way with your doctor or university lecturer. You may adopt a more formal approach when you speak to those in more powerful positions. If you met someone for the first time in a formal situation such as a job interview, you would not use an informal style of communication with them because this would be completely inappropriate and you would probably not secure the position for which you had applied. Now think about the way in which you communicate with your parents; you would probably not communicate with them in the same way that you would speak with a friend. There are unspoken rules to communication and you will have picked many of these up subconsciously during your life without explicitly being taught them.

Static register

This is a 'frozen register' in that there are very specific, fixed ways of speaking in certain situations. An example of this is the way in which communication is played out during legal proceedings. Specific words and phrases are spoken in very specific ways by the judge, solicitors and the jury. When the Lord's Prayer is spoken, it is done in a very specific way. The style of the communication is fixed in these situations and the wording does not alter.

Formal register

A formal register is used in specific formal contexts. In a graduation ceremony the Chancellor or Vice-Chancellor of the university or other official representatives will speak in quite a formal way to the audience. In religious ceremonies, faith leaders will speak formally to their congregations. This form of communication tends to be impersonal and is adopted during speeches, presentations, announcements and sermons. It is a form of communication which is used between strangers.

Consultative register

This is a standard form of communication normally used in professional discourse. It is the way in which a doctor and patient or teacher and student should speak to each other. It might also be used in counsellor/client relationships. This form of communication is used when there is an expert/novice relationships between the two people who are holding the conversation. There is an element of formality and professionalism but the dialogue is often friendly but professional.

Casual register

This form of communication is the form that takes place between friends. It is often informal and is characterised by the use of slang, vulgarities, frequent interruptions or colloquialisms. This form of communication is often evident in letters to friends or written communications on social networking sites. It may be characterised by a 'group language' where members of a social group share a particular style of social language.

Intimate register

This is a private language mainly reserved for close family members or people who are intimate. It is a highly informal language which is private and known only to two people or a social group and it may include verbal and non-verbal forms of communication.

CASE STUDY

Hedgehog Primary School

A primary school was situated in a socially deprived area. Over several years the parents and adults working in the school had got into the habit of using a casual register with each other. The professionals working in the school felt that this was one way of breaking down barriers with the parents. Many of the parents had negative experiences of education from their own schooling and they did not value education. There was significant poverty in the area and many of the parents had serious social issues to address in their own lives. A new head teacher came to the school and she was appalled at the casual register which was used between the parents and the professionals who worked in the school. She sent a newsletter out to the parents which reminded parents to speak to adults in school only in ways which were appropriate.

Critical questions

» Was the head teacher right to tackle the issue in this way?

» What are the advantages of teachers and parents conversing with each other using a casual register?

» What are the disadvantages of teachers and parents conversing with each other using a casual register?

» What are the advantages and disadvantages for teachers and parents using a consultative register?

Various registers of communication differ in their complexities and the regularity of syntax and grammar. The formal register, for example, may be characterised by spoken language which is grammatically accurate. In contrast, communication in the casual register may be characterised by grammatically incorrect spoken language. It is important to note that register is not associated with the speaker but rather with the social and professional contexts in which the conversations take place. You will vary your register dependent upon who you are speaking to, and judges, faith leaders, chancellors and vice-chancellors will certainly use a casual register when speaking to their friends or family members or an intimate register when speaking to their partners.

Teaching children about register

It is important that very young children are taught that they should vary the way they speak according to who they are speaking to. Some of the children that you teach will come from families in which parents use a more consultative register. This is quite important, particularly for very young children, because they need to learn that there is an expert/novice relationship between them and their parents. Sometimes parents and children may jump from using a consultative register to using a casual register and the intimate register may be used from time to time. The register will vary depending on the context, ie the situation, the topic of conversation and the location of that communication. As children get older, particularly as children reach adolescence, parents may start to adopt a more casual register. Many adolescents can cope with this well and they recognise the boundaries that exist between them and their parents. However, some children may exploit this and use it as an opportunity to minimise power differentials between the parent and the child.

Some children may start school having only ever been exposed to a casual register. Their conversations may be characterised by colloquialisms, slang and vulgarities. These children will need to be explicitly taught about the rules of communication. School is a professional context; children come to school to learn from their teachers and other adults. They do not come to school to form friendships with these adults. They need to be taught that there is a specific way of conversing with adults and that this will differ from the way that they communicate with their friends, for example when they are out on the playground or when they play with their friends in different social contexts. Fundamentally, children need to be taught that they will speak differently in the classroom even to their peers compared to the ways in which they speak to their peers in the playground, because the formality of the classroom and its purpose necessitates different forms of communication. They need to be taught that even if they alter the way they speak to their peers depending on whether they are out on the playground or in the classroom, the way in which they converse with their teachers and other adults in school should always be consistent, ie using a consultative register.

If children do not learn to use different registers of speech for different purposes in different contexts then they are at a fundamental disadvantage when they leave school and enter the world of work. They might not keep a job for very long if they use a casual or intimate register with their boss, for example. They need to learn that there is a more formal way of communicating with strangers or people in more powerful positions compared to the casual and informal conversations that they have with their friends. You would not speak to the Queen in the same way you speak to a friend, and children need to recognise this from the very beginning of their education, otherwise they will get into bad habits.

Role play

Role playing familiar situations can help children to learn about register. Scenarios could be created in the classroom in which children have to practise the rules of communication using a consultative register. These could include:

*   visiting the doctor;

*   visiting the vet;

*   role playing teachers and pupils;

*   visiting the bank;

*   paired improvisation, for example, Red Riding Hood talking to her mother.

In these role-play scenarios children would be supported through their conversations through the use of a *talking frame*. This could be a sheet of prompts which scaffold the pupils' talk. Adults play a critical role in modelling spoken language in role play. You could model how to hold conversations in these situations with a teaching assistant through the explicit use of team teaching.

Children will invariably need more support in using the consultative register than the casual register. They often use the casual register naturally because that's what they use with friends. However, problems occur when children start to use a casual register in more formal contexts or with people in a more powerful position, because this can indicate disrespect.

Critical question

» *How might you use drama/role play to encourage children to speak more appropriately in these contexts?*

Use of standard English

It should be noted that standard English is not limited to a specific accent and it covers most registers. The aim of the national curriculum is for all children to use standard English in both spoken and written language. As a trainee teacher, you will need to make a conscious effort to speak and write in correct standard English when you are in school. If your mentor identifies a weakness in your spoken or written language, try not to feel that they are personally attacking you. After all, it is important to remember that communicating in standard English is part of the Teachers' Standards. This is because you are a role model and children will copy what you say and write. It is not about altering your accent and it is certainly not about speaking using a 'posh' voice; it is a matter of making sure that your grammar is correct when you are speaking. Common mistakes include:

* *'Who is sat quietly on the mat?'* rather than *'Who is sitting quietly on the mat?'*.

* *'You have done it lovely'* rather than *'You have done lovely work!'* (Brien, 2012).

* *'I am* **stood** *next to the door'* rather than *'I am standing next to the door'*.

Although it is accepted that people alternate between standard and non-standard English depending on who they are speaking to and the particular context in which the conversation takes place, standard English tends to be used in formal situations where clarity of expression is required. Children also need to be able to write in standard English. It follows that if children are unable to speak in standard English their written expression may also be affected. It is important to correct children when they use non-standard English in situations which require the use of standard English. However, this must be addressed sensitively in order to protect the child's self-concept. One way of doing this sensitively without directly correcting children is to rephrase what they have said to you by providing them with the correct model of standard English.

Modelling register

Adults in school need to model communicating effectively with each other. Schools are professional, working environments, so adults need to converse with each other using a consultative register. When you next go into school, observe the way adults communicate with each other.

* Are they polite to each other?

* Do they listen to each other?

* Do they maintain eye contact?

* Do they wait for the person who is speaking to finish before responding?

* Do they wait their turn or do they 'butt into' conversations?

As a teacher, you are a role model of communication. You therefore need to consider how you interact with all adults in school and with parents. Your communications with parents should be professional and use a consultative register. They should not take place using a casual register. Next, take some time to observe how adults interact with children in conversations. Do they communicate using standard English or do they slip into a casual register by using colloquialisms, incorrect grammar and slang? Observe the way that adults interact with children in the classroom and on the playground. Is the consultative register consistently being applied or do adults slip into using the casual register in more informal situations? Observe the register that is being used in assemblies. Is there evidence that a more formal register is being used in this context?

High expectations

We have spent a considerable amount of time in this chapter discussing registers of speech. This is because we believe that it is important and helps to maintain appropriate professional boundaries between teachers and children.

CASE STUDY

Email communication

A recent email from a student teacher made me think carefully about expectations. The email was set out in the following way:

Hey Jonathan

Thanx for my feedback on my assignment. I worked my balls off for that mark and I am so knackered now. You are a star.

Love

S XXXX

At the risk of sounding like an old fuddy-duddy, I was quite annoyed. The student did respect me as a lecturer (I think) but somehow thought that this was an appropriate form of communication to send to a lecturer. This raises a number of important critical questions.

Critical questions

»   *As a trainee teacher, how would you feel if one of your pupils communicated to you in this way?*

»   *Should the gap between the teacher and the pupil narrow the older the pupil gets?*

»   *Is this just a sign of the times?*

»   *If student teachers do not understand the use of register, what are the implications of this for their own professional practice?*

CASE STUDY

Aspirations Centre

A group of trainee teachers undertook a two-week experience placement in a primary pupil referral unit called *Aspirations Centre*. Although they were well prepared for this experience by their initial teacher training provider, some of them struggled to come to terms with some of the behaviours they observed in the unit. When they returned to the university they reported that they had observed pupils frequently swearing at the teachers and other adults. However, while this was to be expected, they had not expected the adults to swear at the pupils or to speak to them in a casual manner and this had been a frequent response from the adults. Together, we reflected on this and discussed whether the adults had responded appropriately to the pupils.

Critical questions

» What are the advantages of teachers communicating with pupils with social, emotional and behavioural difficulties using a casual register?

» What are the disadvantages of teachers communicating with pupils with social, emotional and behavioural difficulties using a casual register?

» Can the use of a casual register between teachers and pupils with social, emotional and behavioural difficulties help to break down barriers, or is it inappropriate?

Rules for communication

Generally, pupils and teachers in school should use a professional discourse which indicates the nature of the expert/novice relationship. Additionally, within the classroom context, pupils should speak to each other using a consultative register because they are in a formal setting. Establishing some simple rules for communication in the classroom with your pupils will act as a useful frame of reference. These could include the following.

• Wait your turn if someone is speaking to the person you want to talk to.

• Start your conversation with a polite phrase such as 'please' or 'excuse me' then say something.

• Allow the person you have spoken to to give a response.

• Look at the person who is speaking and listen to what they are saying.

• At the end of the conversation, thank the person for talking to you.

These can be adjusted depending on the age of the pupils, but having clear rules helps to demonstrate high expectations and it gives the pupils a framework to follow to support their spoken language.

Activities to develop spoken language

Discussions

Very young children can be supported in having discussions in a range of ways. These include discussion:

- about texts they have listened to or read;
- about how to solve a problem;
- about their ideas for a story;
- in role play/drama;
- which arises as part of a collaborative activity, for example in mathematics or science.

This is not an exhaustive list, but it is important to point out that discussions should take place across the full breadth of the curriculum and not just in English. They should be explicitly planned into lessons so that pupils have opportunities to talk about their learning. Good learners collaborate through high-quality discussion. Some teachers may be reluctant to plan discussion tasks in mathematics, science, history and other subjects because of the lack of recorded evidence which they may feel is necessary. However, it is important to remember that Ofsted inspectors look for evidence of learning taking place in lessons, not just evidence of children's written outputs, and much learning arises from discussions. Discussion as an approach to learning and teaching reflects a socio-constructivist model of learning and the work of Vygotsky (1978), who argued that children learn through social interaction and the use of language. You might need to start by organising children in pairs to undertake paired discussion in the initial stages and then gradually increase the size of the groups. You will need to teach the pupils the rules of discussion. These include:

- waiting your turn before speaking;
- not interrupting;
- looking at the speaker;
- thanking the speaker for their contributions;
- building on what other people have said.

Critical questions

» *Do you learn through discussions? Give some examples.*

» *What are the advantages of planning discussions into your lessons?*

» *What are the associated risks of using discussions in lessons?*

Debates

Very young children can be taught the rules of a good debate. Within the context of a debate, there are usually two contrasting viewpoints. Children will initially need to be supported through the process of taking part in a debate, but once they are familiar with the process and rules, they can gradually take increasing ownership of their own debates. The following structure might help you.

- Introduce the debate, particularly the two opposing views.

- Divide pupils into two groups. One group will discuss arguments *for* and the other group will discuss arguments *against*.

- Give the pupils thinking time, and time to orally rehearse what they are going to say.

- Allow them to plan their responses and teach them how to make notes to support their talk.

- Allow one group to speak and put forward their arguments while the other group listens to them.

- Allow the other group to speak putting forward the contrasting arguments.

- Resolve the debate by having a class vote and synthesise by concluding that *Most people in class X think...*

The ability to participate in debate and respect the opinions of others, even when we disagree, is one of the essential attributes of an educated and civilised human being. It is imperative to teach children that different people have different opinions but that we should respect people's viewpoints even if we do not agree with them. It is important to set some ground rules. These include:

- not interrupting others when they are speaking;

- not ridiculing the opinions of others;

- listening to what others have to say;

- being prepared to change your viewpoint if someone convinces you of theirs

- stating a reason for your opinions.

These can be phrased in child-friendly terms and you can remind the children about these rules at the start of the lesson. A good debate cannot be rushed and the children need thinking time and time to talk through and orally rehearse their ideas. The quality of the lesson will largely be determined by the quality of the debate which takes place, the richness of the discussion, the quality of the arguments being put forward and children's participation, immersion and obsession in the debate.

With children in Key Stage 1 you can use children's fiction and non-fiction texts as a stimulus for debate. Traditional stories can result in some effective debates including:

- *Did Jack do the right thing by selling the cow? (Yes/No)*

- *Was the wolf telling the truth in the True Story of the Three Little Pigs? (Yes/No)*

- *Did Goldilocks do the right thing by breaking into the bears' house? (Yes/No)*

You also need to think about how debates can then be integrated across the curriculum. Examples include:

- *Was it right that children had to work down the mines in Victorian times?* (history)

- *Should we only be allowed to have one car per family?* (geography)

- *Should farmers sell their land for house building?* (geography)

- *Should animals be kept in zoos?* (science)

Critical questions

» *Should children in Key Stage 1 debate controversial issues in society? Explain your answer as fully as possible.*

» *How will you teach children to handle conflicting opinions?*

» *How can you link debate into class themes or topics?*

» *When organising a debate, should children be forced to take a standpoint with which they disagree?*

» *How will you organise the pupils into the groups for and against?*

» *What additional debates could you introduce in those subjects mentioned above?*

Further activities to develop spoken language

The following activities have been taken from Glazzard and Stokoe (2013) *Teaching Systematic Synthetic Phonics and Early English* (Northwich: Critical Publishing).

Puppets

Puppets are a useful way of encouraging children to orally retell stories. They can be placed on an interactive display which gives children access to the text and to an audio-recording of the story. Children can then use the puppets to talk through the story, working in pairs or individually. They can be encouraged to use different voices for different characters.

Listen and tell

Your pupils need to listen carefully as you tell them a new story. Then ask the children to work with a partner to retell the story they have heard. The retelling should contain as much detail as possible. One of the children should begin to retell the story to their partner. On a given signal, the second child continues to retell the story from the point at which the first child stopped. This turn-taking sequence continues until the story is complete. As the children work, you must listen carefully, noting their ability to recall the events of the story in sequence, the story plot and the use of some story language, although you would not expect children to use exactly the same words used in the original story. They need to listen carefully to both the story and to their partner to continue the story.

I hear with my little ear

In this game, children are totally reliant upon what they hear and have no visual cues to support them. Again this is a useful activity for children working in pairs. The speaker (one of the children) must communicate clear information while the listener is only able to ask questions to further clarify their understanding. This activity can be used in a range of ways and the following is only one example of the effective use of this strategy. The children should sit on either side of a screen or back to back. The speaker carefully describes an object and as they do so the listener must draw what is described. The aim of the game is for the listener to identify the object that the speaker has described.

Collaborative story

In this activity, a story is developed with a partner or a group of peers. In partner work, the first child must verbalise either a word or a phrase which the second child then adds to. The children continue taking turns to add either a single word or phrase to create a story. This requires children to listen carefully to one another so that they can ensure that the story they have created makes sense.

Story maps

In this activity, children will illustrate the key events in a story. You will begin to read a story, emphasising that the children must listen carefully. At a specific point in the story you stop and give children time to illustrate what they have heard. Continue and stop again so that the children can add further illustrations. For young children it is beneficial to present them with a simple blank story map to ensure that the illustrations are drawn in the correct order. At the end of the story-telling you should engage the children in retelling the story by referring to their drawings.

Give me a ring

As you introduce children to this activity you must stress the importance of clear communication. The benefits of facial expressions and body language will be withdrawn and understanding will be heavily reliant on the use of language and effective listening skills. This activity is particularly successful when carried out with a partner. The children sit back to back and take turns in discussing a topic or event. They must listen carefully to one another, respond to one another and take turns in conversation.

Critical points

» *Accurate spoken language is essential for writing development.*

» *Good listening skills are essential for reading.*

» *Children need to be explicitly taught about using different registers in their spoken language.*

» *Teachers need to provide good models of spoken standard English.*

» Teachers need to provide opportunities for pupils to use spoken language across the curriculum.

» A silent classroom is not a learning classroom.

Chapter reflections

This chapter has emphasised the importance of explicitly teaching children about the need to adapt their spoken language according to the audience, topic, purpose and location. Children need to be taught how to converse with a range of different people in a range of formal and informal settings and you cannot assume that they will simply assimilate this by osmosis. The importance of teachers being good role models of spoken standard English has also been emphasised. It is important that you model correct spoken vocabulary and that you correct children's use of non-standard English in situations where this is not appropriate.

Taking it further

Alexander, R J (2008) *Towards Dialogic Teaching: Rethinking Classroom Talk* (4th edn). York: Dialogos.

References

Brien, J (2012) *Teaching Primary English*. London: Sage.

Office for Standards in Education (2012) *Moving English Forward: Action to Raise Standards in English*. Manchester: Ofsted.

The Communication Trust (2010) www.thecommunicationtrust.org.uk (accessed 30 November 2014).

Vygotsky, L (1978) *Mind in Society*. London and Cambridge, MA: Harvard University Press.

2 Developing spoken language: Key Stage 2

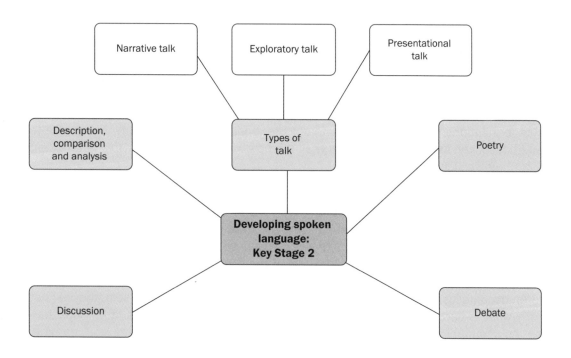

Teachers' Standards

TS3: Demonstrate good subject and curriculum knowledge

Trainees must:

- have a secure knowledge of the relevant subject(s) and curriculum areas, foster and maintain pupils' interest in the subject, and address misunderstandings.

National curriculum links

The programmes of study for English in Key Stage 2 state specific requirements for pupils to discuss what they are learning and to develop their wider skills in spoken language. They must be assisted in making their thinking clear to themselves and others. Across the key stage pupils should become more familiar with and confident in using language in a greater variety of situations and for a variety of audiences and purposes. Their enjoyment and mastery of language should be extended through drama, formal presentations, debate and performance.

Introduction

This second chapter on spoken language moves on from a focus on register and standard English to explore 'finding a voice' through which to communicate understanding, ideas and opinions. It looks at the functions of oral language and the different types of talk that children must master not only to converse in all forms of literacy, but also to be successful learners – to be 'makers of meaning'.

As the Bercow Review (2008) stated *'Speech, language and communication underpin achievement'* and are imperative if children and young people are to succeed as members of society. This followed recommendations made by Rose in the *Independent Review of the Teaching of Early Reading* (2006) that led to the focus turning towards understanding that *'talk is arguably the true foundation of learning'* (Alexander, 2006, p 9). Our capacity to learn has its foundations in our ability to communicate, and, in a literate society, being able to move from spoken to written language is vital. It is how we will be taught and to a large extent how our 'intelligence' will be measured.

Talk in many learning environments has been criticised for being too directive, with the teacher dominating rather than facilitating learners to develop their own competencies. However, the role of the teacher in supporting the development of thinking and oral language is vital. If we consider Vygotsky's theory of cognitive development through interaction with a more able other, where the child works in the zone of proximal development (cited in Wood, 1998) then the size of the group working with a teacher also becomes vital. Often children become lost in large classes. They cannot focus on what is being said, they cannot identify what is pertinent, and likewise, what they have to offer becomes little more than noise. As communication ceases so does the two-way process of teaching and learning, and so we will explore how it is important to guide our children in 'talking groups' just as we would in reading and writing.

Types of talk

We need to be more specific about what we mean by 'talk'. Children need what Alexander describes as a *'repertoire of learning talk'* (2006). There are, after all, a wide variety of purposes and audiences for talk, just as with writing. We use our language to narrate, explain, imagine, compare, describe, evaluate, question, persuade, entertain and much more. The mastery of language for different purposes and audiences is far from simple and your role is to teach, model and prompt your children to explore these 'voices' as you support them towards independent use.

Critical question

» *Between getting up this morning and reading this sentence how many of the types of language outlined at the bottom of the previous page have you used?*

It is useful to distinguish two functions of talk, according to whether the speaker's attention is primarily focused on the needs of an audience, or whether he or she is more concerned with sorting out his or her own thoughts

(Barnes, 1992, p 126)

Exploratory talk

Exploratory talk enables us to rehearse, examine and clarify our ideas. It is the language of interaction and coming to an understanding about an event or situation. We are very good at focusing on this in the early years. Nursery and Reception classrooms are full of exploratory talk; it is at the heart of early years practice. It continues into Key Stage 1, but the demands of the curriculum can bring pressure to bear on limiting the time that is given to really focusing on explicitly teaching for it. This raises the question of whether teachers expect 'presentational talk' far too early, without allowing the child time to explore thoughts and rehearse appropriate means of communicating them before responding. Without time to practise and restructure, the child is faced with the constant possibility faced by all novices of 'getting it wrong'. It is imperative to allow children time to be enveloped in exploratory talk, talk that is not only their own, but shared with others. If we are to explore language we can't do it in isolation. All deep learning means taking risks and recognising that being 'wrong' is part of the exploration of getting it right through teacher and peer collaboration.

Critical questions

» *Can children talk too much? Are they just wasting time?*

» *Does a focus on speaking and listening slow down the pace of lesson, but speed up the pace of learning?*

Presentational talk

This is where we focus our talk on the needs of an audience, and this will be considered in detail later in the chapter when we focus on discussion, formal presentations, debate and performance. However, it is important at this point to realise that it also encompasses the apparently simple task of answering questions.

When questions are posed in everyday conversations, a response usually comes within less than a second of silence. This is also true of classroom questions. Teachers usually allow about a second for a reply, if none is forthcoming, they take back the conversational floor (Wood, 1992, p 206). This in itself raises many questions.

Critical questions

» *Do we give all of our children enough time to explore answers to questions or do we respond to the first hand that goes up?*

» *What strategies might you introduce to ensure that children are given a fair chance to communicate their knowledge and understanding?*

Narrative talk

Narration is the art of story-telling, of recounting real or imagined events. As with all good teaching, you start from the known and with narration in all its forms. Indeed the word 'narrate' come from the Latin verb *narrare* (from *gnarus* 'knowing'). We begin with the child as expert and the following activities lead you from simple recount through the reconstruction of familiar stories into exploring the role of the narrator in performance. They can be used in either key stage.

Activities to support the language of narration

Sharing circle

Bring an object to the circle (keep the talking group small to begin with to develop confidence and to allow each child a voice) and model talking about it. It should be something that is important/precious to you and that you know a lot about – what it is, where it came from, when you got it, who gave it to you, etc. This activity can be a part of a PHSE lesson or an artefact you have been exploring in history. Encourage the children to ask questions about the object that develop your narrative. The children then share their own objects and narrate what they know.

Simple recount

Although the writing of news is often overused, particularly for those children who believe that news has to be exciting and can feel intimidated by peers who seem to have much more interesting experiences to relate, it is again the place to start in narrating something that is new to an audience. It can be a simple shopping trip – it is the language used that is the focus and again you must model the who, what, where, when and develop the narrative into the why and the how.

This news telling can be developed further by delivering the recount in role to support topics being explored in history or science, for example Florence Nightingale telling of her experiences in the wards at Scutari, or Samuel Pepys telling his news about the Great Fire of London. This latter activity supports the national curriculum requirements relating to conventions – the use of first person in diaries and autobiographies.

Retelling familiar stories

Retelling or reconstructing familiar stories is looked at in more detail in both Chapters 5 and 9 in relation to reading comprehension and writing composition, but here we are focused on the oral acquisition of story language. Pie Corbett (2008, p 3) refers to familiar stories as *'mentor texts'* and it is these *'experienced'* and *'trusted'* texts that introduce us to the language of stories – a language that is quite different from the everyday spoken form. When was the last time you began a simple recount with *'Once upon a time'* or one of your pupils used the repetition of *'I ran and ran and ran'* to describe their experience in the playground at break time? It is a richer language that needs to be modelled and explored. This can be done in many ways and using a range of stimuli and resources to support children working in small groups.

- Using pictures/text extracts/story sticks (see Chapter 6) to sequence and retell the key moments in a story – focus on using the exact language of the text. Each child should take it in turn to tell the same part of the story adding more detailed story language each time.

- As above, but now the children take it in turns to retell different parts of the story.

- Throughout, you should be looking for opportunities to model, prompt and praise the correct use of story language, detail and expression.

Critical question

» *How could you use these strategies to explore the language of non-fiction, eg 'The life cycle of a frog' or 'The water cycle'?*

The role of the narrator

Performance of existing texts or the children's own work becomes an expectation throughout Key Stage 2 and the role of story-teller or narrator of known stories is again a good place to start. We explore intonation and the rhythms of speech in more detail later in this chapter and again in Chapter 4, but for now we are focusing on the language and role of the narrator. In its basic form, the narrator acts as the intermediary between the text and the audience and retells the story – they are removed from the action and do not look to affect the observers' conclusions or experience. This is simply adding a performance element to the 'retelling activities' explored above. However, the narrator can be used to 'direct' the audience's understanding of the story; they can add perspectives. Consider, if Little Red Riding Hood narrates her story it will be very different from the tale narrated by the Big Bad Wolf. The language of viewpoint and persuasion can be explored as the narrator becomes part of the action and steps in and out of role.

Description, comparison and analysis

We now move to considering the language of description, comparison and analysis, which takes us from what we know to what we think. When we describe an object or character we start with what our senses tell us are facts about the given focus: what the object looks, feels or smells like or the appearance and actions of a character. The 'wanted poster' activity in Chapter 6 is an example of using the language of description to express our literal understanding of a written text, and this ability to express literal knowledge in spoken language must be a key focus to support our language development. We then move on to comparison, where we explore the differences and similarities between two or more people or things. This attention to detail leads us into analysis, where we look closely at the detail and explore step by step how something is constructed or how an action or impact is achieved.

Activities to support the language of description

Sharing circle

You can use the idea of the sharing circle here too, but with a focus on children using their senses to describe in detail what they know about the object.

Talking pictures

Give each child the same illustration and allow them time to explore it individually. Then ask each member of the group to tell one thing they know from looking at the picture, eg *There is a man wearing a bowler hat / He is standing beneath a large clock*. Return to the picture and, taking one of the descriptive statements, ask the children to add more detail, eg *There is an old man wearing a battered bowler hat / He is stooped beneath a large clock that shows the time is 12 o'clock precisely*. Model extending the vocabulary used and the detail given.

This activity can be extended into the language of the imagination by going beyond what can actually be seen – the children can make assumptions about what they think has happened before the picture was taken (they must give reasons for their ideas) or they can predict what they think might happen next (again giving reasons).

Character study

Select a page or event in a story that depicts a key moment for a character or characters. Begin by modelling a description of the character in terms of what they are doing or saying, eg *Mr Thomas ran into the classroom and he pushed the door closed behind him. He looked around him and sat down heavily in his chair*. Have the children describe the same character and encourage them to explore alternative vocabulary to describe the same scene, eg *Mr Thomas stormed into the classroom and he slammed the door behind him. He peered around him and collapsed onto his chair*. As they explore the different words they can use, the children are developing their understanding of shades of meaning and the impact language choice can have.

Critical question

» *How could you extend this activity by adding action and dialogue? Could you use Freeze Frame (or Tableau, see Chapter 11) to explore character interaction? How would this help the children move into the language of comparison and cause and effect?*

Activities to support the language of comparison

Spot the difference

Select two pictures that are related in some way. This may be through location, event or characters. The children should work in pairs to explore their given picture. They should then describe their picture to another pair (to begin with, the children may need to be supported by being able to see each other's illustrations), who then describe their picture. The pairs should then take it in turns to identify one thing that is the same and one thing that is different about their pictures. Make sure you model the language of comparison. *This picture is the same / there are similarities*, etc.

Characters meet

Begin with stock characters from traditional stories and explore how they are the same and different, eg Goldilocks and Little Red Riding Hood. Have the children work in two groups, with one group taking on a character each. Have them record the main character's traits or the experiences of their chosen subject. Set up a screen or space in which they must stand to present statements about their characters. They take it in turns to share a statement about their character, eg Goldilocks says, *'In my story I visited a cottage in the woods'*. The other group identify a similarity and one of them joins Goldilocks as Red Riding Hood: *'That's where we're the same... In my story I visited a cottage in the woods'*. If the next statement is another similarity then both characters remain on the screen, but if it shows a difference then that character leaves the space, eg Goldilocks says, *'The cottage was empty'* and Red replies, *'Oh no, the cottage was definitely not empty!'*.

Develop this by taking characters from different genres or traditions who nevertheless share particular traits or experiences, eg Robinson Crusoe and Kensuke's Kingdom.

Activities to support the language of analysis

Barrier games

Barrier games involve two children working together, one as the describer/instruction giver and the other as the listener/questioner. The children should be sitting opposite one another with a barrier between them. The first child gives clear instructions to enable the second child to complete a task. The second child can ask questions to clarify understanding and gather more information. They work together to analyse step by step how something is constructed or achieved. Barrier games are often found in Early Years and Key Stage 1, but they are very effective activities for older children and can be made more challenging by choosing tasks that require specialised vocabulary or the exploration of more complex pictures and materials. Here are some examples:

- assembling objects or pictures from a choice of component parts, eg a character's face;

- placing shapes/objects onto a positional grid;

- constructing 3D models;

- following routes on maps/filling in street names and buildings/plot lines;

- completing a step-by-step drawing on a specific subject, eg a house.

It is the clarity of the instructions given and the relevance of the questions asked that lead to successful outcomes, and you will need to model this precision.

Critical question

» *There are, of course, many other types of talk that have not been considered in this chapter and that can be explored across the curriculum. Can you think of effective practical language activities to promote hypothesising in science or evaluating in PE?*

Discussion

Discussion is the action or process of talking about something in order to reach a decision or to exchange ideas. From an early age in school we ask children to work in groups where they must engage in negotiation and discussion. This may result in the production of a piece of work, the solving of a problem or the presentation of some findings. But do we give them the tools to succeed? Do we teach them the ground rules of such dialogue and give them explicit and supported opportunities to practise them? We touched upon some of the rules of dialogue in Chapter 1, but it might be useful to review them here:

- making eye contact with the speaker;

- everybody having a turn in speaking;

- one person speaking at a time;

- speaking in a clear voice;

- using appropriate vocabulary;

- being clear about what you mean and supporting with evidence;

- using the language of reasoning, eg *I think, because, therefore*;

- responding to the other speaker;

- using questions to clarify understanding;

- making extended contributions;

- using facial expressions and gestures.

In discussion, children need to be active both as speakers and as listeners. They must actively include and respond to all members of the group and learn to criticise constructively, but also respond appropriately to criticism of their own views and opinions. You may know many adults who are unable to achieve this.

To explore the language of discussion, children must learn to take on many different roles including leader, negotiator, reporter and observer. An effective way to give children the practice that they need is to introduce them to the jigsaw method, an example of which follows.

Jigsaw method

Choose the topic to be discussed: in this case it is related to a mixed Year 5/6 class and their study in history of the Vikings and their struggle with the Anglo-Saxons for control over the Kingdom of England up until the time of Edward the Confessor's death in 1066.

Home groups

The class is split into groups of four to six and each is given a specific area to research (this occurs during the history lesson), eg Anglo-Saxon homes/methods of warfare/farming. They are given time to become 'experts' in their chosen field and make notes and share findings. During the next English lesson they begin in their home groups where they discuss their specific area. They are reminded of the ground rules for discussion. They negotiate and agree three important points or facts that they will focus on in the next part of the jigsaw. (The different stages in this strategy should not be rushed and can be spread over a series of lessons, according to the experience of the children.)

Expert groups

The children are now placed into 'expert groups' with one from each of the home groups. Again the ground rules for dialogue are reviewed. To give purpose to the discussion they are put into role as Vikings who have been sent on a fact-finding mission by their leader and are given specific questions to consider, for example:

*   Would it be easy to conquer the Anglo-Saxons in battle?

*   Would the Vikings be able to live in Anglo-Saxon homes?

Adequate discussion time is given before the teacher interjects in role as the Viking leader asking for advice and information to support plans for an invasion. Again, time is given for group discussion before specific questions are asked, and the groups are given time to prepare a formal piece of advice about the invasion.

Throughout this 'jigsaw', the language of discussion is constantly modelled and reviewed. Each session is monitored by an observer, one child (a different one each time) who sits on the edge of the group and uses a check sheet to record which ground rules are used well and which are being neglected. The observer should be instructed to be constructive and record evidence to support their observations. Particular ground rules such as making extended contributions and responding to what others say may be highlighted for particular attention. After each discussion, the observer gives feedback to the groups on their application of the rules and individual children are encouraged to discuss how they are developing their discussion skills.

Critical questions

» *How does the role of the observer support the development of discussion?*

» *What does the observer gain from their role in the discussion?*

» *How might an observer be used to promote the development of other types of talk?*

Debate

Discussion can naturally lead into debate, the language of persuasion. A debate is a formal discussion on a particular matter in a public meeting in which opposing arguments are put forward and which usually ends in a vote. Again, this idea was introduced in Chapter 1, but here are the structure and rules of a serious debate.

1. A topic is chosen.

2. Two teams line up to put their case.

3. The proposer puts forward a motion and argues the case for passing/agreeing with the motion.

4. The opposer argues the case against the motion.

5. Two more speeches follow, one from the proposing team and the other from the opposing team.

6. The debate is opened up to the audience, who ask questions of both teams.

7. Having answered the questions, each team sums up their arguments.

8. The motion is put to the vote where it is either accepted or rejected.

For a fun and informative step-by-step guide to debating and understanding this giant game of verbal ping-pong, look out for *How to Debate: An Introduction* on YouTube, where a Lego-based film leads you through the steps to successful debating (see Taking it further).

It is important to note that children must learn to debate from different viewpoints and so explore different perspectives. They do not always get to argue for what they truly believe in. This, after all, is the exploration of persuasive language and you need to model strategies and language that will win them the vote. Examples are:

Pathos	Big names	Data
Using emotional language to make people sympathise or empathise with the argument	Using names of experts or people with influence. In school this may be the headteacher or popular members of staff	Using graphs and charts and language such as 'as you can see'

Here are some phrases and words that need to be modelled and taught for different purposes:

- to illustrate a point: *for example, namely, such as;*

- to make suggestions: *keeping this in mind, therefore;*

- to link information: as a *result, similarly, additionally;*

- to contrast points: *on the other hand, nevertheless, in spite of;*

- to conclude or summarise: *because of this, with this in mind, in short.*

Children in upper Key Stage 2 love a good argument and so it is important that you give them something to get their teeth into. Here are some good topics for debate.

- Are video games good for you?

- Are there aliens?

- Are vampires real?

- Is peer pressure beneficial or harmful?

- What's the importance of the Olympics?

- Will computers replace teachers?

Debates can, of course, be structured around any curriculum subject area, from science to geography, and are particularly suited to PHSE.

Critical question

» *What motions can you think of for each of the curriculum subjects?*

Poetry

As a trainee teacher, you need to know as much about poetry as you do about stories (Medwell et al, 2014, p 156). This might surprise you, but if you consider the new curriculum for English you will see that poetry has a high profile across the key stages in the programmes of study for both reading and writing. Later in this book we explore the ways in which reading and composing poetry enable children to further develop their comprehension skills and consider how it promotes fluency, which in turn supports word reading and ultimately, language comprehension.

However, this chapter is about spoken language and the role poetry has in developing a feel and enjoyment of playing with sounds and words. When we read and perform poetry we can begin to really hear that sound conveys meaning. Babies respond to the sounds their parents make long before they ever understand the meaning of the individual words. In the same way, young children and indeed second-language users learn songs and rhymes through latching on to the rhythms, rhymes, pitch and phrasing of the verse (all of these terms will be explored further in Chapter 4). In any language we can often recognise when the speaker is afraid or angry by the way in which the words are expressed, and it is this universal communication that makes poetry so accessible. Added to this is brevity; poems are often short, and while few of us can learn a book off by heart, we can memorise many short poems. There is also the question of convention and the very fact that many poetic forms do not demand an understanding of sentence construction allows even the earliest speaker to participate.

Make sure to give your children frequent opportunities to 'play with sound' through poetry. Make yours a poetry-friendly classroom, where poems are the norm rather than the exception. Have a poem of the day, have poems displayed on walls or play a recording of a poem to welcome children in the morning. Below are some ideas to facilitate the oral exploration of poetry.

Activities to support poetry

Echo valley

Have the children seated/standing in two rows facing one another. Introduce the idea that between them lies a deep valley and they must communicate with each other through echoing sounds, words and phrases. To begin with, give the children the words or phrases they are to echo, but as the children become more experienced, allow them to lead. Play with the way in which words might be repeated or the volume might be explored. Extend to lines from songs and poems.

Call and response

Introduce call-and-response songs such as 'Boom Chicka Boom' or 'A Keelie'. These are ideal for warming up voices and developing confidence in 'performing'. To begin with, you will lead the call as the children respond, but, again, as they become more confident, give different groups and individuals this responsibility. The children can move on to create their own call-and-response verses.

Itch and scratch

This activity involves adding actions to words and, while being good fun, it also helps children memorise by association. Initially collect favourite words and pair them, eg *puff* and *pant/sing* and *dance/sneeze* and *cough*. Have the children chant the words and add actions, sometimes just explore the actions and then lead into reciting the words alone. Using appropriate poetic forms, such as the Kenning below, begin to add simple rhythms as the children learn existing poems, using actions to aid their memory.

The following Kenning expresses many of the attributes of poetry:

> *A Mind Stretcher*
> *A Word Builder*
> *A Convention Breaker*
> *A Memory Maker*
> *A Rhythm Section*

Critical points

» *Talk is the foundation of learning.*

» *Teachers must give children the opportunity to develop exploratory talk before asking them to engage in presentational talk.*

» *Children need to be allowed to work in 'talk groups' to develop confidence and find their voice.*

» *Children need to acquire a 'repertoire of talk' for different purposes and audiences – teachers need to teach and model these different types of talk.*

Chapter reflections

This chapter has explored many of the different demands we place upon children if they are to become successful oral communicators. Success in spoken language underpins achievement in all areas of English. In our day-to-day experience, listening, speaking, reading and writing do not exist in isolation, but rather work alongside each other to form an integrated whole – the big picture of language. Throughout the book, you will see us returning to the same questions and goals as the different areas of the English curriculum are explored. We enrich children's understanding and enjoyment of language when we give them opportunities to combine oral and written language for meaningful purposes.

Taking it further

Brien, J (2012) *Teaching Primary English*. London: Sage.

Wilson, A (2005) *Creativity in Primary Education*. London: Learning Matters (Sage).

www.singup.org (accessed 30 November 2014)

English Debate, Lego Style: https://uk.video.search.yahoo.com/video/play?p=english+debate+lego+style (accessed 30 November 2014)

References

Alexander, R J (2008) *Towards Dialogic Teaching: Rethinking Classroom Talk* (4th edn). York: Dialogos.

Barnes, D (1992) The Role of Talk in Learning, in Norman, K (ed) *Thinking Voices: The Work of the National Oracy Project*. London: Hodder & Stoughton.

Bercow, J (2008) *A Review of Services for Children and Young People (0–19) with Speech, Language and Communication Needs*. London: DCFS Publications.

Corbett, P (2008) *Good Writers*. A National Strategies publication. [online] Available at: www.foundationyears.org.uk/files/2011/10/Good_Writers1.pdf (accessed 17 October 2014).

Medwell, J A, Wray, D, Moore, G E, and Griffiths, V (2014) *Primary English: Knowledge and Understanding* (7th edn). London: Learning Matters (Sage).

Rose, J (2006) *Independent Review in the Teaching of Early Reading: Final Report.* Nottingham: DfES.

Wood, D (1992) Teaching Talk: How Modes of Teacher Talk Affect Pupil Participation, in Norman, K (ed) *Thinking Voices: The Work of the National Oracy Project,* London: Hodder & Stoughton.

Wood, D (1998) *How Children Think and Learn: The Social Contexts of Cognitive Development.* Oxford: Blackwell.

3 Word reading: Key Stage 1

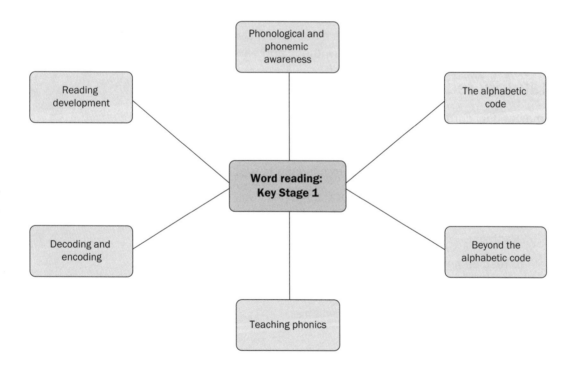

Teachers' Standards

TS3: Demonstrate good subject and curriculum knowledge

Trainees must:

- have a secure knowledge of the relevant subject(s) and curriculum areas, foster and maintain pupils' interest in the subject, and address misunderstandings;

- if teaching early reading, demonstrate a clear understanding of systematic synthetic phonics.

National curriculum links

Word reading

The national curriculum states that:

> It is essential that, by the end of their primary education, all pupils are able to read fluently, and with confidence, in any subject in their forthcoming secondary education.
>
> (DfE, 2013, p 15)

The national curriculum states that a *systematic* approach to phonics should be adopted in the early teaching of reading to unskilled readers when they start school. It is interesting to note that the document does not refer to a *synthetic* approach to phonics teaching, which has driven policy in initial teacher training and in schools in recent years. However, the Teachers' Standards explicitly state that teachers must have a clear understanding of *systematic synthetic* phonics, which indicates that a synthetic approach to phonics is statutory.

Statutory requirements

In the national curriculum (DfE, 2013) pupils in Year 1 should be taught:

- to apply their phonic knowledge as the route to decode words;
- to respond speedily with the correct sound to graphemes for all 40+ phonemes;
- to identify alternative sounds for graphemes;
- to read accurately by blending sounds in unfamiliar words containing grapheme–phoneme correspondences that have been taught;
- to read common exception words;
- to read words containing –s, –es, –ing, –ed, –er and –est endings;
- to read words of more than one syllable;
- to read words with contractions;
- to read aloud books which are consistent with their developing phonic knowledge;
- to reread books to build up fluency and confidence in word reading.

In the national curriculum (DfE, 2013) pupils in Year 2 should be taught:

- to apply their phonic knowledge as the route to decode words until automatic decoding has become embedded and reading is fluent;
- to read accurately by blending the sounds in words that contain the graphemes taught so far, recognising alternative sounds for graphemes;

- to read words of two or more syllables;

- to read words containing common suffixes;

- to read common exception words;

- to read words quickly and accurately without overt sounding and blending, when they have been frequently encountered;

- to read aloud books closely matched to their phonic knowledge, reading unfamiliar words accurately, automatically and without undue hesitation;

- to reread books to build up fluency and confidence in word reading.

Although the requirements for Year 1 and Year 2 appear to be similar in many respects, there is a clear focus on developing fluency in reading in Year 2 and an expectation that pupils will be able to read words automatically without an undue focus on overt sounding and blending. The focus in Year 2 is on developing accurate and speedy word-reading skills. In Year 1 there is a clear focus on establishing the skill of blending phonemes for decoding new words but with an expectation that pupils will move away from *overt* sounding and blending once they have encountered a word several times. Pupils who do not begin to develop fluency/automaticity with word reading should be given additional support to help them develop this.

Introduction

With good teaching, all pupils can learn to read, regardless of social background, special educational needs or ethnicity. This expectation should be embedded in all schools and in all initial teacher training programmes. Pupils who do not learn to read are effectively disenfranchised because the skill of reading is essential to participation as a full member of society (DfE, 2013). As a trainee teacher, you need to take seriously your responsibility for teaching children to read. All teachers are teachers of reading and your training should provide you with the underpinning knowledge and skills to help all children to learn to read. Reading is too important to be marginalised and all primary teachers should prioritise the teaching of reading in their daily timetable to give pupils the best opportunity to succeed. Phonics alone will not solve the problem of underachievement in reading. Pupils need access to a broad and rich language curriculum (Rose, 2006) and regular opportunities to apply their phonic knowledge and skills. Pupils also need opportunities to read a wide range of texts for meaning and for pleasure.

Learning to read is time limited and needs to be mastered as quickly as possible so that pupils can access the rest of the curriculum. Reading is a tool for learning. Once the important skill of learning to read has been mastered, pupils can then begin to *read to learn*. It is through reading that pupils develop their skills of learning independently. It allows them to develop their knowledge and understanding across the full breadth of the curriculum, thus advancing their cognitive development. It is also a tool for facilitating communication. The growth of technology in recent years has meant that forms of communication are increasingly diverse. As well as communicating through speech, we now communicate through text messaging, email and via social networking sites. However, all of these forms of communication rely on us being able to read quickly and accurately. We live in a society in which we are surrounded by print. Our ability to process this print into meaningful forms of communication is essential for our full participation in a literate society. Reading enables us to function in our daily lives, communicate with each other and learn independently. It also gives us enjoyment by taking us into imaginary worlds which are far removed from the realities of our day-to-day lives. This deepens our imagination, extends our vocabulary and provides immense pleasure.

One of the aims of the national curriculum is for pupils to read easily, fluently and with good understanding. Additionally, teachers must ensure that pupils develop the habit of reading widely and often, both for pleasure and information. Reading will help pupils to develop a wide vocabulary. The national curriculum emphasises the importance of pupils learning to read through a systematic phonics approach, particularly at the beginning stage of learning to read. However, there is a significant focus on developing fluency in reading so that pupils avoid the overt sounding out after several encounters with a word. The focus is on developing automaticity so that pupils learn to read accurately and fluently, even in the early stages of learning to read.

Understanding the terminology of reading

Throughout this chapter, specific terminology is used which you need to understand in order to evidence TS3. Full definitions are provided in the glossary at the back of this text to avoid repetition.

Reading development

Pupils generally start school with good *linguistic* comprehension (Johnston and Watson, 2007). This means that although they tend not to be able to read printed words, they do understand much spoken language. Understanding language is critical to being an effective reader. After all, the purpose of reading is to gain meaning from print. Reading is the product of being able to recognise words on a page (word recognition) and being able to understand language. The Simple View of Reading (Gough and Tunmer, 1986) is a conceptual framework which reflects this by breaking down reading into two distinct components:

- word recognition: decoding (sounding out and blending) printed words;
- linguistic comprehension: the ability to understand spoken language.

To become effective readers, pupils need to develop both the skills of word recognition and language comprehension. Although both skills are developed concurrently, teachers initially need to place greater emphasis on developing the skill of word recognition. This is because pupils will not be able to gain any meaning from text which they are unable to decode unless the text is read aloud to them.

The national curriculum (DfE, 2013) states that a phonic approach to word recognition should be emphasised in the early stages of reading development because it is essential that children understand that letters on a page represent the sounds in spoken language. While beginning readers are developing their skills in word recognition it is essential that adults support their comprehension by engaging them in dialogue about the text and drawing the child's attention to the illustrations. This is because the child initially focuses on decoding words at the expense of comprehending the text. As their skills in word recognition improve, the child will be able to focus less on overtly sounding out words, and word recognition becomes more automatic, giving the child more opportunity to focus on their comprehension of the text.

The Simple View of Reading is useful because it enables teachers to assess a child's skills in each of the two domains. Some pupils, including pupils with dyslexia, may have good linguistic comprehension but may be poor at word recognition; these children understand spoken language but struggle to make grapheme–phoneme correspondences or to blend phonemes together to read words. Others have good word recognition skills but very poor linguistic comprehension; these pupils can read words on a page but they struggle to understand what they are reading; they often appear to be 'barking' at print. Some pupils are weak in both domains and effective readers are strong in both.

This model helps teachers to decide how to support pupils with reading difficulties. Children with good linguistic comprehension and poor word recognition may require a phonics intervention. Those pupils with poor linguistic comprehension and good word recognition may require a language comprehension intervention. A child who is weak in both domains may need a phonics intervention programme and a language comprehension intervention programme because a phonics intervention alone will not sufficiently address the weaknesses in linguistic comprehension.

Critical questions

» *How will you use the Simple View of Reading to identify the needs of poor readers?*

» *How will you decide which type of intervention is appropriate for your poor readers?*

» *How will you monitor the effectiveness of any interventions you implement?*

Additionally, the Simple View of Reading helps teachers to recognise that developing pupils' skills in each domain requires different *types* of teaching. The national curriculum is explicit that word recognition skills should be taught through access to a systematic phonics programme in which phonic knowledge is developed progressively by following a clearly structured approach to introducing the alphabetic code. Historically, there was a view that decoding printed words was largely unimportant (Goodman, 1973) because it was thought that skilled readers did not need to read all the words on a page. At the time it was considered that it was more important to understand the meaning of the text from the context rather than reading every word accurately. However, research evidence has now demonstrated that guessing words from context is what *unskilled* readers do (Johnston and Watson, 2007). Children will make greater progress in reading if they have a strategy for working out unfamiliar words (Johnston and Watson, 2007). Although some children are able to recognise words as whole-word shapes by committing them to memory, this approach does not help them to read words that they have not seen before. The phonics approach, in contrast, provides children with a strategy for working out unfamiliar words. Once word recognition becomes automatic, children can then focus to a greater extent on the skill of linguistic comprehension.

Critical questions

»   *What type of teaching is needed to develop children's skills in word recognition?*

»   *What type of teaching is needed to develop children's skills in linguistic comprehension?*

As a trainee teacher, it is important that you understand how children develop as readers. Understanding models of reading development will help you to identify what stages children have reached and what their next steps are. This will help you to plan suitable learning opportunities to advance their reading development. However, the problem with developmental frameworks is that they over-simplify the learning process when in reality learning is quite complex. Learning to read is a complex process, but once it is mastered we read with automaticity and make it look simple. When children are first learning to read they have to focus on several skills: sounding out the phonemes; blending phonemes together to read words; moving across a line of text from left to right; moving onto the next line and so on. It is hardly surprising that they lose the meaning of the text; they are focusing on all the technical aspects of reading. We can help them to keep a sense of the text by engaging them in dialogue about it. Once these skills become embedded and automatic, children can then focus less on them, leaving them more 'brain space' to focus on the plot, the characters and the description.

Ehri's model (Ehri, 2005) of sight word reading is well established and encompasses the thinking of major theorists. In examining children's reading development, Ehri found that children progress through four phases. These are summarised below.

Pre-alphabetic phase

Ehri found that very young children rely on visual cues to help them read words. At this phase, children are very aware of print in their environment. They can read logos (such as *Cadbury's* or *Coca-Cola*) because they learn to recognise the word within the context in which they normally see it. They draw on cues such as colours, shapes and sizes of letters to help them to recognise words they see in the environment, and if these cues are removed and the word is presented in normal print, children generally cannot recognise it (Johnston et al, 1996).

Partial alphabetic phase

At this phase, children start to use their knowledge of the alphabet to attempt to read words, although they do not work all the way through the phonemes in a word from left to right (Johnston and Watson, 2007). They may overly focus on the initial phoneme within a word, for example by reading *bin* as 'boy'. They are making use of some phonic knowledge at this phase but often it results in inaccurate word reading. Poor readers tend to arrest in their reading development at this phase (Romani et al, 2005) and these pupils often benefit from access to a multi-sensory phonics programme taught at a much slower pace than traditional synthetic phonics programmes. Very able poor readers, such as those with dyslexia, may adopt a visual rather than alphabetic approach to reading (Johnston and Morrison, 2007). In view of Ehri's model of reading development, all pupils whose development is arrested at this phase need further support to help them master the alphabetic code and its application in reading.

Full alphabetic phase

At the full alphabetic phase, children are able to make connections between the letters and phonemes all the way through a word. When presented with the letters t-a-p at this phase a child can say the corresponding phonemes in sequence to read *tap*. As children start to develop knowledge of *digraphs* (two letters representing one sound) they can sound out words such as *throat* by saying and blending the phonemes represented by the corresponding graphemes from left to right through the word, in this instance /th/r/oa/t/.

Consolidated alphabetic phase

At this stage, children start to recognise morphemes (units of meaning), for example by combining them to read whole words. Children also start to recognise *rimes* within words rather than needing to break words down into smaller graphemes. They then start to use their knowledge of rimes to read words by analogy.

Phonological and phonemic awareness

Phonological awareness is the ability to identify syllables, onsets and rimes within words. Children with good phonological awareness are able to identify rhyming strings. They can hear the /at/ sound in *cat* and are able to substitute onsets to go in front of the rime to generate new words (*rat/sat/mat/bat*). They are able to identify the odd one out in a series of rhyming words and they are able to hear syllabic divisions within words. Bradley and Bryant (1983) reported a strong correlation between children's ability to recognise rhyme and their subsequent development as good readers. This illustrates the importance of immersing children in rhyme from a very early age through access to nursery rhymes, rhyming games and rhyming stories.

Phonemic awareness is the ability to perceive and manipulate the phonemes in *spoken* words (Johnston and Watson, 2007). A child with good phonemic awareness would be able to tell you that *mat* has three sounds (/m/a/t/) and that *coat* also has three sounds (/c/oa/t/). Children with good phonemic awareness are able to hear the sounds in a *spoken* word in the correct sequence from left to right all through the word.

Smallest meaningful units of sound

In synthetic phonics, words are broken down into the smallest meaningful units of sound as follows:

flag	/f/l/a/g/
grass	/g/r/a/ss/
boat	/b/oa/t/
crisp	/c/r/i/s/p/
spray	/s/p/r/ay/
duck	/d/u/ck/

snail   /s/n/ai/l/
string   /s/t/r/i/ng/ (ng is a *consonant digraph*)
chop   /ch/o/p/ (ch is a consonant digraph)

This means that consonant blends such as *bl/cl/cr/dr/sp* are not taught because they can be broken down further into their separate sounds. Instead they are taught as *adjacent consonants* (two consonants which make two separate sounds).

Sound buttons

The use of sound buttons can be helpful to encourage children in the early stages of learning to read to focus on each separate grapheme in a word and its corresponding phoneme. Examples are given below.

d	o	g	
.	.	.	
s	t	o	p
.	.	.	.
c	oa	t	
.	—	.	

Enunciation of phonemes

In synthetic phonics you should always use the pure sound (or soft sound) by pronouncing it without the schwa: this is an extra sound or unstressed vowel which is sometimes added onto phonemes. It is very easy to add an 'uh' sound to the end of phonemes. For example, 'c' in the word *cat* should not be pronounced '*cuh*'. Pronouncing the sound clearly and precisely will make the process of blending sounds together much easier.

Teaching phonics

The *Independent Review of the Teaching of Early Reading* (Rose, 2006) advocated the synthetic approach to phonics as *'the best and most direct route'* (2006, p 4) into early reading. The approach emphasises the importance of teaching children to blend phonemes all through the word for reading and additionally emphasises blending as the prime approach to reading. It is taught at a rapid pace and the process of blending is applied to the text almost from the very start of the programme after enough grapheme–phoneme correspondences have been taught to build words. This contrasts with analytic phonics where pupils were once taught using onset and rime (for example *br-ush*).

Although some (eg Wyse and Goswami 2008) have questioned the claims made about synthetic phonics, the evidence that underpins synthetic phonics is compelling (Johnston and Watson, 2004) and has demonstrated that children taught using synthetic phonics made better progress in their reading compared to children taught using analytic phonics.

Critical questions

»   *Do you think synthetic phonics will eradicate reading failure?*

»   *Is one approach to teaching reading suitable for all children?*

»   *If pupils are still not developing good word recognition by Key Stage 2 is a synthetic phonics intervention programme appropriate for them, given that this approach has not helped them learn to read in Key Stage 1?*

Multi-sensory approaches to teaching phonics

Rose (2006) emphasised that multi-sensory activities were a feature of high-quality phonics work. However, he did question the idea that people can be categorised into a single learning style and argued that children often approach a task through a range of sensory pathways. We therefore recommend that you plan each lesson to provide children with opportunities to learn through visual, auditory or kinaesthetic pathways. Multi-sensory approaches could include:

*   activities involving physical movement, for example tracing letter shapes in the air or on the floor;

*   segmenting using magnetic letters;

*   writing in a range of media including sand, glitter, salt, shaving foam;

*   using software on the interactive whiteboard;

*   making letter shapes out of malleable materials;

*   writing graphemes or words in mud.

CASE STUDY

Multi-sensory teaching

Emily, a trainee teacher, decided to make her phonics lessons more interesting by teaching some of the lessons outside. In one lesson she set up large trays of sand, rice, glitter and shaving foam in the outside space. Graphemes that had been previously taught were positioned around the walls and fences. Emily started the lesson by shouting out the phonemes which represented the graphemes on the wall and the children demonstrated their phonic knowledge by running to the appropriate graphemes. She then introduced the new grapheme–phoneme correspondence that she wanted the children to learn in the lesson – *ai-/ay/*. Emily had written some words on the floor using chalks. These words included words such as *hail, pain, jail, snail, rail, nail,* and *wait.* After saying the word, the children had to stand next to the correct spelling. She pointed out that the grapheme normally occurs in the middle of the word. Emily then asked the children to choose which tray they wanted to use in this lesson to practise their skills of segmenting. She shouted out words that included the grapheme–phoneme correspondence, including *again/plain/rain/drain,* and the children were asked to attempt to write the words in the media they had selected. Using large words on separate pieces of card, the children were then asked to put the words in the correct order to make a sentence. The sentence included words which included the new grapheme.

Critical questions

» How did Emily maximise pupil participation in this lesson?

» How did Emily plan assessment for learning opportunities into this lesson?

The alphabetic code

In English we represent the sounds of spoken words by letters, and the alphabetic code shows the graphemes that represent each sound of speech. Various versions of the English alphabetic code are available and it is recommended that you display an alphabetic code chart in your classroom so that children begin to associate each of the sounds of speech with their corresponding graphemes.

The simple alphabetic code

In the simple alphabetic code, children are introduced to one grapheme (letter or group of letters) for each sound of speech. Although there are 26 letters of the alphabet there are not enough letters to represent all the sounds of speech (phonemes). This means that letters are grouped into two (digraphs) or three (trigraphs) to represent all the sounds of speech. In the simple code, each phoneme is represented by one spelling variation, which may be one letter or two or more letters. There are 40+ phonemes in the English language and each one is represented by a spelling variation (or grapheme).

The complex alphabetic code

In the complex code, children are introduced to the different spelling variations (graphemes) that represent a sound. Thus, the sound /ue/ can be represented by 'oo' (spoon), 'ew' (flew), 'u-e' (tune) or 'ue' (true). Additionally, one grapheme can represent various phonemes. For example the grapheme 'ch' represents different sounds in in church, champagne and chemist.

Key concepts you must understand

Concept 1: Sounds (phonemes) are represented by letters (graphemes). English is an alphabetic language – unlike Mandarin Chinese, for example, where whole words are represented by character.

Concept 2: A phoneme can be represented by one letter (grapheme) or by a group of two or more letters. For example, 'th', 'igh', 'ear' each represents a single phoneme.

Concept 3: The same sound (phoneme) can be represented (spelt) more than one way: **c**at; **k**ite; **ch**emist.

Concept 4: The same grapheme (spelling) may represent more than one phoneme: dr**ea**m–d**ea**f; fr**ow**n–bl**ow**n; f**ie**ld–tr**ie**d.

Concept 5: The split vowel digraph:

> In the word *name* the **a-e** grapheme represents one unit of sound which is enunciated as /ay/. Therefore this word is decoded as /n/ay/m/.

> In the word *pine* the **i-e** grapheme represents the sound /igh/ so this word is decoded as /p/igh/n/.

Critical question

» *Phoebe is a child in a Reception class. You introduce the new sound for today which is /f/ represented by the grapheme 'f'. Phoebe suddenly shouts out 'My name starts with an f'. You have not yet started looking at alternative graphemes for this sound because you are focusing on developing your pupils' understanding of the simple alphabetic code. How do you respond in this instance?*

Decoding and encoding

When pupils *decode* text they translate the graphemes into sounds and they merge (blend) these sounds together all the way through the word in sequence in order to read the target word. When pupils *encode* or *segment* a word they translate the spoken word into symbols (Brien, 2012) by identifying the constituent phonemes that make up the word and translating these into the corresponding graphemes, either through writing or selecting the appropriate symbols. Decoding and encoding (blending and segmenting respectively) are reversible processes.

Critical questions

» *Do the skills of blending and segmenting develop at the same rate? In your next placement school, work with a small group of children and assess their ability to decode and encode a set of words.*

» *What are the advantages and disadvantages of decoding? Substantiate your arguments with academic literature.*

» *What are the disadvantages of teaching children to segment words? Are there any perspectives in the literature in relation to this?*

» *What evidence can you find in research studies that support phonics approaches to reading compared to approaches which do not rely on phonics?*

The national curriculum (DfE, 2013) explicitly states that pupils should read books which are closely matched to their developing phonic knowledge. This gives pupils the best chance of successfully decoding print. Even if the words presented in the text are unfamiliar, pupils should, theoretically at least, have the necessary phonic knowledge to be able to success-fully tackle them through sounding out the phonemes and blending them together to identify the target word.

Critical questions

» *What are the advantages of decodable texts?*

» *What are the disadvantages of decodable texts?*

» *Can you find any literature to support your arguments?*

Beyond the alphabetic code

Exception words

The national curriculum (DfE, 2013) refers to 'exception words'. These are words that have an unusual correspondence between the spelling and the sound. An example of an exception word is *said*, because the sound in the middle of the word is /e/ although it is represented by the letters '*ai*'. The phonics scheme that your school uses will identify the different exception words that need to be taught at specific phases. When teaching children to read exception words, then, it is logical to draw their attention to the part of the word that is tricky because this will help them later with spelling these words.

Reading words with suffixes

In Year 1, children need to be taught to read words with suffixes by building on the root word that they can already read. In Year 2, the whole suffix should be taught as well as the letters which make it up.

Syllables

In Year 1, children should be taught to read words of more than one syllable that contain taught grapheme–phoneme correspondences. In Year 2, pupils should be taught about syllable boundaries and how to read each syllable separately before combining them to read the words.

Critical points

» *Children need to be taught phonics through a systematic approach.*

» *In the simple alphabetic code one sound (phoneme) is represented by one spelling variation (grapheme).*

» *In the complex alphabetic code one phoneme can be represented by different graphemes.*

» *In the complex alphabetic code one grapheme can represent more than one phoneme.*

» *In synthetic phonics blending is the prime approach for reading print.*

» *Blending and segmenting are reversible processes.*

» *Pupils need access to a broad and rich language and literacy curriculum which includes opportunities to read a wide range of texts as well as books which are within the scope of children's phonic knowledge.*

Chapter reflections

Rose (2006) was clear that quality early teaching of phonics includes the use of rich multi-sensory approaches which engage children in learning. Many of the academic critiques of phonics have focused on how phonics can lead to pupils becoming disengaged with reading. The case studies provided in this chapter illustrate that phonics lessons can be exciting if children are taught using visual, auditory and kinaesthetic approaches. However, phonics is not the end of the story. Children need to apply the skills they are learning in phonics to their reading and writing, and teachers need to focus on the application of phonics just as much as they focus on teaching children phonics. If pupils are not taught how to apply their phonic knowledge to the task of reading and writing then there is little point in teaching phonics in the first place. Phonics is only a tool to support writing and reading and therefore the success of your phonics teaching should be judged by the impact that teaching has on developing pupils as readers and writers, not on the basis of your phonics lessons per se.

Taking it further

Glazzard, J, and Stokoe, J (2013) *Teaching Systematic Synthetic Phonics and Early English*. Northwich: Critical Publishing.

Johnston, R S, and Watson, J (2005) *The Effects of Synthetic Phonics Teaching on Reading and Spelling Attainment: A Seven Year Longitudinal Study*. [online] Available at: www.scotland.gov. uk/Resource/Doc/36496/0023582.pdf (accessed 6 August 2014).

References

Bradley, L, and Bryant, P (1983) Categorising Sounds and Learning to Read: A Causal Connection. *Nature*, 301: 419–21.

Brien, J (2012) *Teaching Primary English*. London: Sage.

Department for Education (DfE) (2013) *The National Curriculum in England: Key Stages 1 and 2 Framework Document*. London: DfE.

Ehri, L C (2005) Development of Sight Word Reading: Phases and Findings, in Snowling, M J and Hulme, C (eds) *The Science of Reading: A Handbook*. Oxford: Blackwell, pp 135–54.

Goodman, K S (1973) The 13th Easy Way to Make Learning to Read Difficult: A Reaction to Gleitman and Rozin. *Reading Research Quarterly*, 8: 484–93.

Gough, P B, and Tunmer, W E, (1986) Decoding, Reading and Reading Disability. *Remedial Special Education*, 7: 6–10.

Johnston, R, and Watson, J (2007) *Teaching Synthetic Phonics*. Exeter: Learning Matters.

Johnston, R S, and Morrison, M (2007) Towards a Resolution of Inconsistencies in the Phonological Deficit Theory of Reading Disorders: Phonological Reading Difficulties Are More Severe in High IQ Poor Readers. *Journal of Learning Disabilities*, 40: 66–79.

Johnston, R S, and Watson, J (2004) Accelerating the Development of Reading, Spelling and Phonemic Awareness. *Reading and Writing*, 17(4): 327–57.

Johnston, R S, Anderson, M, and Holligan, C (1996) Knowledge of the alphabet and explicit awareness of phonemes in pre-readers: the nature of the relationship. *Reading and Writing*, 8: 217–34.

Romani, C, Olson, A, and DiBetta, AM (2005) Spelling Disorders, in Snowling, M J and Hulme, C (eds) *The Science of Reading: A Handbook*. Oxford: Blackwell, pp 431–47.

Rose, J (2006) *Independent Review in the Teaching of Early Reading: Final Report*. Nottingham: DfES.

Wyse, D, and Goswami, U (2008) Synthetic Phonics and the Teaching of Reading. *British Educational Research Journal*, 34(6): 691–710.

4 Word reading: Key Stage 2

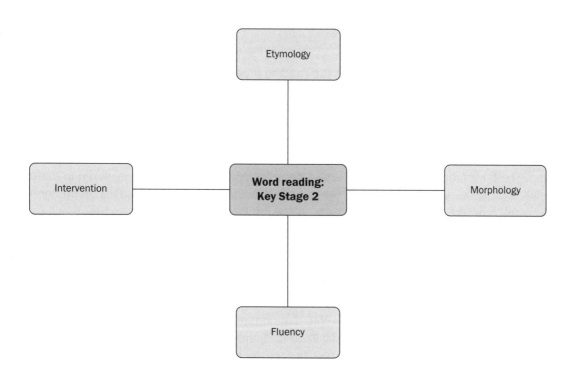

Teachers' Standards

TS3: Demonstrate good subject and curriculum knowledge

Trainees must:

* have a secure knowledge of the relevant subject(s) and curriculum areas, foster and maintain pupils' interest in the subject, and address misunderstandings.

National curriculum links

Statutory requirements

The statutory requirements state that pupils in Years 3–4 should be taught to:

- apply their growing knowledge of root words, prefixes and suffixes (etymology and morphology) as listed in English Appendix 1 in the national curriculum, both to read aloud and to understand the meaning of new words they meet;

- read further exception words, noting the unusual correspondences between spelling and sound, and where these occur in the word.

The statutory requirements state that pupils in Years 5–6 should be taught to:

- apply their growing knowledge of root words, prefixes and suffixes (etymology and morphology) as listed in English Appendix 1 in the national curriculum, both to read aloud and to understand the meaning of new words they meet.

Introduction

Chapter 3 introduced the complexity of the reading process and focused on the importance of equipping children with the decoding and encoding skills they need to become successful readers and writers, including how words must be blended and segmented using phonemes, the smallest units of sound. This chapter explores breaking words into morphemes – the smallest units of meaning. Linked to this search for meaning is the understanding of the etymology of the English language and how recognising the origins of words aids us in reading them. The terms root, prefix and suffix have been introduced and are now explored in more detail. Children need not only to know 'what' to do in technical terms but also to comprehend 'why' and 'how' the functions of words are altered and enriched by the parts that make up the whole. Alongside word reading there must also be fluency, a complex concept that is closely examined later in this chapter.

It cannot be stated too often that reading is a necessary life skill in our print-rich society and the failure to acquire this skill has lifelong consequences.

Figure 4.1 is based upon research (KPMG Foundation, 2006) undertaken to review the long-term consequences of literacy difficulties for individuals and society and the financial costs that result. The research shows that the 'costs' begin with interventions, permanent exclusions and truancy prosecutions and extend into unemployment and pressures placed on the National Health Service. Beyond these are the worrying statistics showing that a large percentage of the prison population have poor basic skills. Of course, the costs are not purely financial and have major implications for low self-esteem and communication. When looked at from this perspective you will see how vital your role is in giving every child their chance to become an expert reader, not only in terms of basic life skills, but also in opening up exciting new worlds and knowledge.

Figure 4.1 *Long-term consequences of literacy difficulties*

Etymology

Word reading is not so much about 'learning words' but 'learning about words'. In Key Stage 2 there is an emphasis on children using their etymological knowledge to understand the meaning of the new words they meet. So what is etymology? This is how it is defined in Appendix 2 of the national curriculum:

> A word's etymology is its history: its origins in earlier forms of English and other languages, and how its form and meaning have changed.

Modern English has been influenced by several core languages, in particular Anglo-Saxon, Norman French, Latin and Greek. All of these languages have their own conventions and perhaps this explains why there is always 'an exception to the rule'. The English language is extremely inconsistent and the same sounds of speech can be represented by more than one grapheme. Other languages have a more consistent relationship between the sounds of speech and their corresponding graphemes. English is more complex and demands that readers make choices and use rules both to pronounce words and identify meaning. Exploring this complexity does not have to be hard work and is perhaps best approached through analogy – see Gina Cooke's great example of peeling an onion and the unexpected roots of the word onion itself on YouTube (see Taking it further). The study of etymology should be fun and investment in some good etymological dictionaries is a must for making historical and geographical links. Remember you will have to model how to use and read these dictionaries before the children can work independently.

Activities to support the study of etymology

Around the world in 80 words

Give the children a map of Europe or the world and a list of words. Ask them to label the countries from which the words originate and match the words to the countries. Use an etymological dictionary both to locate the origins of the given words and to find new examples, eg *xylophone* (Greek), *bayonet* (French), *umbrella* (Latin).

What do you notice?

Divide the children into pairs and give them a set of cards to sort into words from different language origins. Ask them to discuss and explore what these words appear to have in common, eg *umbrella, tarantula, confetti, domino* (Latin); *scheme, chorus, chemist, echo* (Greek), or how they came to enter the English language, eg *bungalow, dinghy, jungle, pyjamas, shampoo* (Hindi/Urdu).

Timeline

Provide the children with a timeline, eg AD 100 – Roman occupation (Latin), AD 500 – Angles and Saxons invade Britain (Anglo-Saxon), AD 1200 – Normans conquer Britain (French), and a list of words to place on the timeline. They should then use an etymological dictionary to locate origins and generate their own words to add to the timeline.

Critical questions

»   *How can you link the study of etymology to other curriculum areas such as history, geography, science or foreign languages?*

»   *How can an exploration of local place names make the study of language more personal for the children?*

Morphology

A word's morphology is its internal make-up or structure. Morphology links the study of words with the study of grammar (see Chapter 10) because morphemes, the smallest units of meaning in words, may also indicate how a word functions in a sentence (Medwell et al, 2014, p 61).

At this point it is helpful to define and consider the three possible elements of a word's structure:

Root word	The form of a word after all affixes are removed that can stand alone, eg *help* is the root word in *helpful*
Prefix	A prefix is added at the beginning of a word in order to turn it into another word, eg **over**take, **dis**appear
Suffix	A suffix is added at the end of a word. Suffixes have two functions: they can either create new words, eg thought**less** or change the function of the word, eg *beauty* (noun) – *beautiful* (adjective)

In English there are two types of morphemes.

* **Free morphemes**: these are stand-alone words and can be content words such as nouns, main verbs and adjectives or function words such as determiners, conjunctions and prepositions.

* **Bound morphemes**: these cannot exist in isolation and are almost exclusively prefixes and suffixes.

Prefixes are generally more easily understood as they only have one possible function and that is to create new words. However, suffixes can cause more problems because the reader needs to identify not only a new word, but often a new function in a sentence. Some suffixes are derivational morphemes and change the grammatical category of a word:

* change a noun into an adjective, eg *beauty* – *beautiful*;

* change an adjective into a noun, eg *fearless* – *fearlessness*;

* change a verb into a noun, eg *promote* – *promoter*;

* create verbs, eg *orchest**rate***;

* create adverbs, eg *happ**ily***.

Complicated, isn't it? Now consider inflectional morphemes which assign a particular grammatical property to the word. They act as markers to indicate:

* tense, eg *walk* – *walk**ed***;

* comparison, eg *big* – *bigg**est***;

* number, eg *car* – *car**s***;

* possession, eg *John* – *John**'s***.

All of this morphological knowledge is demanded as you move from teaching Key Stage 1 to Key Stage 2 and it is important to make sure that the children don't just see morphology as adding to the beginnings or ends of words – they need to understand what affixes are doing. Compare Tom's different approaches in the following case study.

CASE STUDY

Tom

At the beginning of the autumn term, Tom was reviewing the use of the past tense with his Year 3 class. The children were inconsistent with both usage and spelling and he wanted to consolidate their understanding before introducing them to the present perfect form of verbs. Tom wrote the suffix 'ed' on the board and gave some examples of sentences written in the past tense – underlining the suffix to be added. He then gave the children a worksheet where they had to change present-tense sentences into the past. The results were disappointing. Many children continued to write words such as 'jumpt' for *jumped*, 'hoped' for *hopped* and 'groand' for *groaned*. A few children struggled to identify the verbs that needed converting and added 'ed' to adverbs, eg 'quicklyed'.

After the previous day's disaster, Tom spent the following series of lessons unpicking the children's understanding of the task. He began by **reviewing** the term 'verb' and what it meant through some quick-fire drama activities that had the children physically exploring verbs. He then **revised** their understanding of the past tense through games relating to today and yesterday. Next he **modelled** changing verbs from the present to the past and vice versa in the context of full sentences. As he did this, Tom **explored** with the children the spelling conventions of doubling consonants after short vowel sounds (eg *chat – chatting*) and dropping the 'e' and adding 'ed' where long vowel sounds were split (e.g. *hope – hoped*). Finally, he gave the children the opportunity to **investigate** different pronunciations (eg *jumped/wanted/called*) to confirm that although they sounded different they all shared the same spelling. The children then repeated the original activity with much better results.

Critical questions

»   *What are the crucial differences between these two lessons? In particular, note why it is important to break the learning down into small meaningful steps and how this supports understanding for both reading and writing.*

»   *How could you use morphology to further children's understanding of shape in mathematics?*

Activities to support the study of morphology

Find your partner

This activity explores compound words and requires two sets of cards each containing one half of a compound word, eg *car – park*. The children are given one card each and must find their partner to create a compound word. This is not always as easy as it sounds and the children may discover that they can find more than one partner. Consider these six words and the number of compound words you might produce: *out, sea, break, play, side, time*. At the end of the exercise, ask the children to define the compound words they have constructed.

New word from old

The English language is constantly growing, with new words being added to every addition of our major dictionaries, such as *screenager, superbad* and *photobomb* (Waugh and Neaum, 2013). Ask the children to use their existing knowledge to write their own definitions of these words before they look them up (probably online, as they may not yet be in the dictionaries you have in school).

My word

As with all of these activities, the emphasis here is on really *understanding* the morphemes that are added to words to change their meaning. Give the children a list of known words that have prefixes and ask them to identify the meanings. For example:

dishonest – *dis* meaning 'not' – not honest;

retell – *re* meaning 'again' – tell again;

autograph – *auto* meaning 'self' – self-written.

The children could then invent their own words, eg *disview/relove/autolike*, and write their own definitions.

Critical questions

» *How could you adapt the above My word activity to explore the study of suffixes, both derivational and inflectional?*

» *If the blending of non-words supports phonological understanding in Key Stage 1 (see the Year 1 phonics check to assess phonic knowledge and support word reading), how does the creation of new words support morphological understanding?*

Fluency

This chapter has continued to explore 'word reading' and the need to orchestrate phonic and morphological knowledge to recognise and process the meanings of words. This is no mean feat, but accurate word reading is an essential skill when mastering the art of reading for meaning. If you consider the following two sentences; *'He sat by the river panting'* and *'He sat by the river painting'*, you can see that just one letter totally changes the meaning. However, accurate word reading on its own does not lead to successful comprehension. If a child reads word by word, in what is often described as a 'robotic voice', without cohesion and fluency, then they will struggle to understand. So what is fluency?

Reading fluency is generally defined as the ability to read text with speed, accuracy and proper expression. Let's begin with the word 'speed'; it is often confused with the word 'fast', not just by teachers, but by the children themselves.

CASE STUDY

Speedy readers

Rizwan believed that to be a good reader he had to be a fast reader and to be really success-ful he had to be the first to finish. Rizwan had a strategy and that was to turn over two pages at a time – as you can imagine, there were a lot of gaps in his understanding.

Jane also embraced the concept of speed – so much so that it totally dominated her 'attack' on print. Her reading could best be compared to a machine-gun being fired as she spat out the words, taking no notice of the punctuation, and fired from one sentence to the next. Reading was a stressful experience with no time for comprehension or self-correction.

Flow

Neither of these children understood that what was actually meant by speed was the 'flow' of their reading. When reading flows it is like a river and its pace speeds up and slows down as the reader adjusts to the needs of the text. This flow is achieved by recognising most words automatically and decoding new ones with relative ease. The reading sounds smooth – it sounds like talking – but to achieve this smoothness, the reader needs to read in phrases. Teachers are often heard encouraging children to be fluent and to read with phrasing, and as expert readers they model this fluency, but do they teach it?

Critical questions

» *Do we explicitly teach fluency in the same way, for example, that we teach phonics?*

» *How might you tackle the teaching of fluency?*

Phrasing

A phrase is more than just a group of words; it is a group of words that have a unified func-tion in a sentence. Each phrase carries meaning. Children need to identify the words that go together, and you need to show them. An activity as simple as cutting a sentence into phrases and asking the child to read each phrase individually and identify its meaning will support a child's understanding of how to identify which words go together. So which words do go together?

- Noun phrase: this is a phrase that tells us the 'who' or 'what' of a sentence, eg
- Who: *the big dog/the big hairy dog/the big hairy brown dog*
- Adverbial phrase: this is a phrase that tells us the 'when', 'where' or 'how' of a sentence, eg
- When: *at midnight/at midnight yesterday evening*
- Where: *along the moonlit path/along the moonlit path behind the palace*
- How: *very excitedly*

If you then add a verb – 'ran' you have the whole sentence: *At midnight yesterday evening, the big hairy dog ran, very excitedly, along the moonlit path behind the palace.*

Good phrasing supports both word recognition and comprehension. Always encourage children with poor fluency to read aloud and listen to themselves – only then will they hear when it doesn't sound right and make sense.

Expression

This is a word full of meaning and complexity. When you ask a child to read with expression what are you asking them to focus on? When you model reading with expression what are you asking them to listen to?

Expression refers to prosody – the rhythm of speech. This rhythm is made up of a number of features.

Intonation (the use of pitch)	This relates to the rise and fall of the voice. It can make the difference between a statement and a question.
Stress	This is the degree of emphasis given to a sound or syllable. In a word it can distinguish between a noun or a verb, eg in the word *permit* if you stress the first syllable it is a noun, but if you stress the second syllable it becomes a verb: ***per**mit/per**mit***. Strong stressed syllables can also convey the meaning of a sentence; the meaning and implications change depending on where the stress is located: HARRY kicked the ball. (not Fred) Harry KICKED the ball. (not threw) Harry kicked the BALL. (not my head)
Tone	The tone of the voice expresses emotion, eg anger, sarcasm, apology.

You will come to know that the amount of correct expression indicates how much the reader comprehends in the text.

Flow, accuracy and expression are the key elements of fluency. The more fluently a child reads, the more they comprehend – the more they comprehend, the more fluent they become. It is vital that you teach for fluency from the beginning with even the most novice reader. What the child knows and has control over should be read smoothly and at speed. Don't accept slow word-by-word reading on texts that are within the child's control. They need to hear themselves as good readers and to achieve this you need to teach fluency through books with which they are familiar. Use texts that the child has already shown they can decode so that all of their focus can be on fluency and comprehension. This will speed up their processing and they will more readily apply their skills of accurate word reading and fluency on new texts.

There is one more word that is crucial to consider if a child is to become a fluent reader and that word is *confidence*. A lack of confidence in anything, whether that be playing a particular sport or singing in public, leads to being tentative, actions may become disjointed and ultimately you may just give up. Giving up cannot be an option in learning to read, and yet many children, even in Key Stage 1, can be heard saying *'I can't read.'* To be confident, a child must taste success and to achieve success it is your job to offer texts that are within their control. This is not a case of giving the children texts that are 'too easy' – a text is only 'too easy' when it ceases to have any challenge. Returning to the idea of familiar books, you can see that you are offering the child a new challenge when they use an already decoded text to develop fluency. They will begin to hear themselves as good readers and will become motivated and confident to broaden the range of texts that they read. Confidence is also linked to enjoyment – if a child is good at something they will enjoy it and seek to do more. Be careful as a teacher that you don't inadvertently remove the 'positive' from reading. Consider the following case.

CASE STUDY

Daniel

Daniel is a child with behavioural issues who often disrupts lessons. This is particularly true when the lessons involve collaboration with other children such as art and PE. David enjoys both of these subjects, but when he begins to argue and disrupt he is often removed from the activity and told *'to get a book and read it in the reading area'*. Only after a set time sitting sullenly flicking through a book is Daniel allowed to return to the original activities.

Critical questions

» *What message is the teacher giving Daniel about reading?*

» *What strategies might you use to reinforce the joys of reading in your classroom?*

» *Why is it important that the children see you as a reader?*

Activities to support voice modulation for fluency

How loud?

Ask the children to sit either in a circle or in two rows facing one another, depending on the situation being explored. Introduce different scenarios to enable the children to explore the volume and pitch of their voices as they pass given messages to one another. For example, when facing one another across a valley they should shout, but hiding from an intruder they should whisper.

Telephone conversation

Split the children into pairs and ask them to act out having a telephone conversation in which they are only allowed to use the words *yes* and *no*. The manners in which they manipulate these words express an idea of the meaning and mood of the conversation, eg sharing a secret, invitation to a party, having an argument. This can be extended by giving the children specific characters and events from a text. For example, they might be Cinderella asking one of the ugly sisters if she can go to the ball.

Just one word

Again have the children working in pairs and give them a scenario such as meeting a friend, falling out and then making up. They are only allowed to use one word throughout the conversation, eg *flannel* or *sausage*. The word itself doesn't matter, but a two-syllable word gives the children more to play with.

Which sentence?

Direct the children to work in small groups and give each group a sentence. They must explore the different ways that this sentence can be expressed and how its meaning changes depending on the word being stressed, eg *I* can't see you tonight / I **can't** see you tonight / I can't **see** you tonight / I can't see **you** tonight / I can't see you **tonight**.

They can also explore saying the sentence as a statement or question or when laughing or sobbing. Extend this exercise by introducing specific emotions and saying it nervously/ angrily/happily, etc.

Character voices

This activity explores the different kinds of voices that best fit certain characters. Begin with stock characters such as giants and wicked witches. Ask the children how they think an 'ugly sister' sounds. What clues are in the text? Then extend into the characters from the books they are reading. How do they think the author intended the character to sound and how does this relate to whether we are sympathetic to the character?

Extracts from text

Give children time to prepare extracts from a text where characters are interacting with one another. Ask them to perform these extracts to other members of the group or class, who act as an active audience and comment on the effectiveness of the voices.

Intervention

By now it will be clear to you that reading is not a simple skill to acquire. Many children arrive in Key Stage 2 with only a tentative control of this necessary skill and this should not be a surprise when you consider the complexity of the process they are learning to master. It is your responsibility to identify the areas in which they are struggling and the gaps that may need to be filled. These holes in their knowledge may be phonic or morphological; they may be related to language structure or fluency and comprehension. The longer the gap is allowed to remain, the harder it is to fix. Like tooth decay, the hole gets bigger and the consequences more disturbing for both you and the child. The most effective intervention is early and specific.

Of course, if children have gaps in their phonic knowledge then they need to be addressed, but it is important to identify why these gaps exist. If it is because they missed the learning through absence then the fixing may be straightforward and the school's phonics programme can be returned to. However, if the problem is that of not processing what has already been taught then a more personalised intervention programme will have to be introduced. There are many interventions available. For a report on the effectiveness of the different schemes, see *What Works for Children and Young People with Literacy Difficulties* (Brooks, 2013).

It is crucial to identify children with specific learning needs and to identify learning styles. For example, many dyslexic learners seem to be visual, kinaesthetic learners who struggle with auditory programmes that work from 'part to whole' (MacKay, 2005). MacKay warns against 'death by phonics' for certain learners who need a mix of phonics and whole-word, visual, strategies. Phonically regular polysyllabic words can be easier for these children to apply their skills to, eg **hospital** is easier to differentiate from **fantastic** than **cat** is from **net**.

This is not an argument against the systematic teaching of phonic knowledge, but rather a reminder that you must see children as individuals who may need different approaches. While the phonics scheme will work for the majority of children, it is no use just repeating it ad nauseam for children with auditory difficulties. As explored in Chapter 3, the most effective teaching is multi-sensory, and this is just as pertinent in Key Stage 2. As Albert Einstein famously said, '*Insanity is doing the same thing over and over again, and expecting different results.*'

If a child struggles to read fluently you must again isolate the main cause – is it poor reading accuracy, limited vocabulary or poor comprehension? Finally, remember the importance of motivation. Motivation is arguably the most critical ingredient for long-term success in learning to read (Lyons, 2003, p 84). It leads to autonomy and when linked with challenge stimulates curiosity and the desire to succeed.

Critical points

» *Word reading is not about 'learning words' but 'learning about words'.*

» *Children need to be introduced to the etymology and morphology of the English language.*

» *It is vital that children understand not only which units of meaning exist in a word, but also why and how they alter the meaning and function of the word.*

» *This knowledge needs to be broken down into small meaningful steps.*

» *Children need to be able to read fluently to be successful.*

» *Gaps in their phonological and morphological knowledge need to be addressed.*

Chapter reflections

Word reading is much more than identifying isolated words, it is about exploring the richness of the English language through its hidden meanings to discover new knowledge. It can be likened to a giant jigsaw that when constructed presents the text's 'big picture'. Phonics, etymology, morphology and oral language structures need to be assembled through explicit teaching and interactive investigations. You should then present opportunities for children to apply their knowledge across the curriculum.

Taking it further

Cooke, G (2012) *Making Sense of Spelling*. [online] Available at: www.youtube.com/watch?v=0mbuw ZKOlr8 (accessed 30 November 2014).

Crystal, D (2007) *Words, Words, Words*. New York: Oxford University Press.

Crystal, D (2011) *The Story of English in 100 Words*. London: Profile Books.

Wolf, M (2008) *Proust and the Squid: The Story of the Reading Brain*. Cambridge: Icon Books.

References

Brooks, G (2013) *What Works for Children and Young People with Literacy Difficulties: The Effectiveness of Intervention Schemes* (4th edn). The Dyslexia-SpLD Trust. [online] Available at: www.interventionsforliteracy.org.uk (accessed 30 November 2014).

KPMG Foundation (2006) *The Long-Term Costs of Literacy Difficulties*. London: KPMG Foundation.

Lyons, C (2003) *Teaching Struggling Readers: How to Use Brain-Based Research to Maximise Learning*. Portsmouth, NH: Heinemann.

MacKay, N (2005) *Removing Dyslexia as a Barrier to Achievement: The Dyslexia Friendly School Toolkit*. Wakefield: SEN Marketing.

Medwell, J A, Wray, D, Moore, G E, and Griffiths, V (2014) *Primary English: Knowledge and Understanding* (7th edn). London: Learning Matters.

Waugh, D, and Neaum, S (2013) *Beyond Early Reading: Critical Teaching*. Northwich: Critical Publishing.

5 Reading comprehension: Key Stage 1

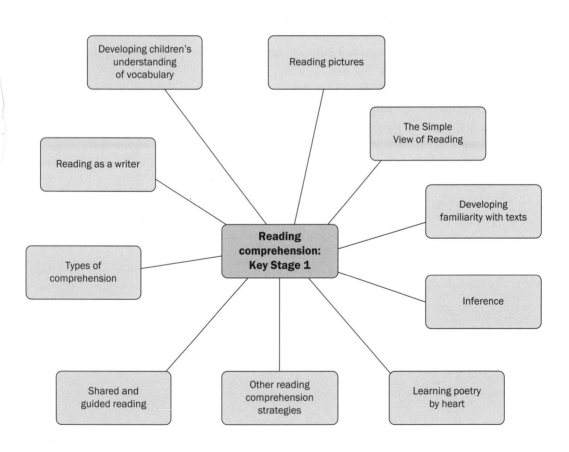

Teachers' Standards

TS3: Demonstrate good subject and curriculum knowledge

Trainees must:

- have a secure knowledge of the relevant subject(s) and curriculum areas, foster and maintain pupils' interest in the subject, and address misunderstandings.

National curriculum links

Reading: comprehension

The national curriculum states that:

All pupils must be encouraged to read widely across both fiction and non-fiction to develop their knowledge of themselves and the world in which they live, to establish an appreciation and love of reading, and to gain knowledge across the curriculum. Reading widely and often increases pupils' vocabulary because they encounter words they would rarely hear or use in everyday speech. Reading also feeds pupils' imagination and opens up a treasure-house of wonder and joy for curious young minds.

(DfE, 2013, p 14)

Statutory requirements

The statutory requirements for reading comprehension for pupils in Year 1 state that pupils should be taught to:

- *develop pleasure in reading, motivation to read, vocabulary and understanding by:*
  - *listening to and discussing a wide range of poems, stories and non-fiction at a level beyond that at which they can read independently;*
  - *being encouraged to link what they read or hear to their own experiences;*
  - *becoming very familiar with key stories, fairy stories and traditional tales, retelling them and considering their particular characteristics;*
  - *recognising and joining in with predictable phrases;*
  - *learning to appreciate rhymes and poems, and to recite some by heart;*
  - *discussing word meanings, linking new meanings to those already known.*
- *understand both the books they can already read accurately and fluently and those they listen to by:*
  - *drawing on what they already know or on background information and vocabulary provided by the teacher;*

– checking that the text makes sense to them as they read and correcting inaccurate reading;

– discussing the significance of the title and events;

– making inferences on the basis of what is being said and done;

– predicting what might happen on the basis of what has been read so far.

• participate in discussion about what is read to them, taking turns and listening to what others say;

• explain clearly their understanding of what is read to them.

(DfE, 2013, p 21)

In Year 2 pupils should be taught to:

• develop pleasure in reading, motivation to read, vocabulary and understanding by:

– listening to, discussing and expressing views about a wide range of contemporary and classic poetry, stories and non-fiction at a level beyond that at which they can read independently;

– discussing the sequence of events in books and how items of information are related;

– becoming increasingly familiar with and retelling a wider range of stories, fairy stories and traditional tales;

– being introduced to non-fiction books that are structured in different ways;

– recognising simple recurring literary language in stories and poetry;

– discussing and clarifying the meanings of words, linking new meanings to known vocabulary;

– discussing their favourite words and phrases;

– continuing to build up a repertoire of poems learnt by heart, appreciating these and reciting some, with appropriate intonation to make the meaning clear.

• understand both the books that they can already read accurately and fluently and those that they listen to by:

– drawing on what they already know or on background information and vocabulary provided by the teacher;

– checking that the text makes sense to them as they read and correcting inaccurate reading;

– making inferences on the basis of what is being said and done;

– answering and asking questions;

– predicting what might happen on the basis of what has been read so far.

- *participate in discussion about books, poems and other works that are read to them and those that they can read for themselves, taking turns and listening to what others say;*

- *explain and discuss their understanding of books, poems and other material, both those that they listen to and those that they read for themselves.*

(DfE, 2013, p 28)

Introduction

This chapter focuses on the importance of children reading for understanding. After all, the purpose of reading is to read for meaning. We emphasise in this chapter that children need a good understanding of language in order for them to develop good reading comprehension and we argue that reading comprehension ability is the product of both good word recognition and good linguistic (language) comprehension. Throughout the chapter we draw on the Simple View of Reading (Gough and Tunmer, 1986) to argue that linguistic comprehension and word recognition should be taught concurrently. However, we argue that in the early stages of reading development, the *emphasis* should be placed on word recognition because pupils cannot understand what they are reading if they are unable to read words in the first place. Although some pupils with poor word recognition skills may be able to understand texts that are read aloud, it is essential that pupils learn to decode in the early stages of development so that they can move from learning to read to reading to learn. This chapter also addresses key strategies for teaching reading comprehension.

Developing children's understanding of vocabulary

Linguistic comprehension starts to develop well before young children even begin to learn to read. Immersing children into a language-rich environment is therefore essential in order to develop their understanding of spoken language and broaden their vocabulary. Bruce (2004) emphasises that *'spoken language makes a huge contribution to how a child makes a start on reading and writing'* (p 179). Developing a good understanding of spoken language lays the foundations of developing good reading comprehension skills in children.

Children who are born into language-impoverished environments are clearly disadvantaged compared to those born into language-rich environments. Such children lack the exposure to the breadth of language that those in language-rich environments experience. Conversations in the home and between parents and children in the natural environment support the development of children's understanding of language. Introducing children to new vocabulary is critical to supporting the development of linguistic comprehension. In the 1970s, Bernstein, an educational psychologist, argued that the oral culture of homes and communities was critical to subsequent achievement in school. Controversially, Bernstein argued that social interaction differed between social classes in the United Kingdom, with more elaborated forms of language being more common among the middle classes (Bernstein, 1971). Bernstein argued that elaborated forms of language are a prerequisite for subsequent educational achievement and that, consequently, children from working-class families were limited in their educational opportunities because of their more restricted language experience (Bernstein, 1971). His work received strong criticism at the time for his lack of observational evidence to substantiate his claims. Academics have also continued to question Bernstein's assumptions by arguing that the problem is not about children's use of language but rather that schools expect children to employ middle-class ways of using language (Lambirth, 2006).

Children born into language-impoverished environments will benefit from an environment in early years settings and in school which is flooded with language. However, a language-rich curriculum benefits all children. Exposure to spoken language provides children with the tools to express themselves and increases the breadth of vocabulary which they know, understand and use. Children will develop their language through having access to rich play-based learning experiences. It is through play that children are exposed to language and social play enables them to use language as a tool for communication. The role of the adult in developing children's language is critical during child-initiated play-based learning experiences. Effective practitioners understand that they have a critical role to play in scaffolding children's learning during play. Through supporting their play, adults can model new language, thus introducing children to a wider vocabulary. This process of scaffolding language enables children to access new vocabulary. This is an example of Vygotsky's *'zone of proximal development'* (Vygotsky, 1978). This theoretical model helps educators to understand how children can move from their *actual* level of development to a *potential* level of development through support from someone who is more knowledgeable.

Effective pedagogy in the early years includes the provision of learning play environments as well as the more adult-directed tasks traditionally associated with the word 'teaching' (DfES, 2004). Excellent early years settings provide children with opportunities to learn through freely chosen play and through teacher-initiated group work (DfES, 2004). Rose (2006) clearly asserted that the teaching of early reading should take place within the context of a language-rich curriculum. He emphasised the importance of helping to develop pupils' communication skills and the need to provide children with co-operative learning experiences in language-rich contexts.

Critical questions

»   *What impact does technology in the home have on children's language development?*

»   *Is there a link between social class and language deprivation? What literature can you find to substantiate your arguments?*

»   *What is the impact of working parents on the oral culture within the home?*

The Simple View of Reading

The Simple View of Reading (Gough and Tunmer, 1986) identifies the two components of reading: recognising and decoding printed words and linguistic comprehension – the ability to understand spoken language. Children will almost certainly struggle to understand the texts they listen to and read if they do not understand and have a wide repertoire of *spoken language.*

The Simple View of Reading demonstrates that *both* linguistic comprehension and word recognition are essential to good reading development. Hoover and Gough (1990) demonstrated how separate measures of word recognition (decoding) and linguistic comprehension together give a good account of how well children can read (Johnston and Watson, 2007). Although both elements are important in developing good reading comprehension, each element needs to be assessed separately in order to determine whether children require intervention within a specific domain.

Each element requires a different kind of teaching but teachers need to focus on both aspects in order to give children the best chance of becoming good readers. However, without good decoding skills, children will not be able to understand what they are reading. It is therefore critical that teachers in the EYFS and in Year 1 place greater emphasis on developing children's skills in decoding. Once this skill is secure and children are fluent in word recognition, teachers will then be able to place greater emphasis on developing their understanding of texts. However, it is important to emphasise that we are not suggesting a linear approach to word recognition and language comprehension. You should not focus exclusively on developing children's skills in decoding before you move onto developing their skills in comprehension. Both skills should be developed concurrently but there will be greater emphasis initially on decoding in order to develop children's fluency in reading.

You need to ensure that as well as focusing on decoding (sounding out and blending), children have opportunities to further develop their language. They need to learn language through being immersed in rich language and social contexts and they need to have opportunities to listen and respond to a wide range of stories, poems and non-fiction texts. The skill of word recognition needs to be taught within a rich language context so that all the time children are being flooded with language. As children focus on decoding texts, it is important that you talk to them about the text that they are reading so that they understand it. You can do this by:

- engaging them in dialogue about the illustrations;
- asking them questions about the text;
- relating the text to their own experiences;
- asking them to predict what might happen next;
- talking to them about the characters.

Initially, children need to focus their energies on sounding out and blending phonemes to read words. At his stage, in addition to supporting them with blending, you might have to do more work than the pupils in terms of comprehension. Once word recognition is secure and fluent you should place more emphasis on the children being able to engage with the text through:

- answering questions where the answer can be directly extracted from the text;
- making predictions;
- making inferences;
- giving a response to the text.

The more children read, the better their linguistic comprehension will be. Introducing children to a wider range of books, poetry and non-fiction texts will extend their exposure to language. This will have a positive impact on their reading comprehension ability. Additionally, children's skills in decoding print will improve the more practice they have through reading.

As a teacher, it is critical for you to understand the reasons that underpin poor achievement in reading. Some children's reading development may be impeded because their skills in decoding are not secure, even though they may have good linguistic comprehension. These pupils require additional support in decoding print through access to a multi-sensory phonics programme. In contrast, some children may be good decoders but have poor linguistic comprehension. Their reading comprehension skills will not improve unless their language comprehension improves and these pupils may therefore need access to a language intervention programme. A child who has both poor linguistic comprehension and poor decoding skills may need a language intervention programme and a phonics intervention. They need support to improve their skills in both domains because reading comprehension ability is the product of both. Effective readers are those who have well-developed language comprehension and fluent word recognition skills. The national curriculum (DfE, 2013) is clear in its expectation that children should start to move away from sounding out and blending as soon as possible so that an over-reliance on decoding does not inhibit children's understanding of the texts they are reading. You therefore need to teach children to decode quickly and accurately and, once they have been exposed to a word several times, they need to develop the skill of saying the word quickly and automatically so that they do not lose the thread of what they are reading.

Types of comprehension

Brien (2012) identifies four different levels of comprehension. These are:

- **literal comprehension:** the ability to extract straightforward information from the text;

- **inferential comprehension:** the ability to search for clues in the text by reading between the lines;

- **evaluative comprehension:** the ability to understand what may be around and beyond the text;

- **appreciative comprehension:** the ability to understand the qualities of the text.

This list demonstrates how comprehension skills gradually increase in complexity with literal comprehension being the lowest level. Comprehension in fiction should provide pupils with opportunities to explore unusual vocabulary and phrasing, imagery and the evocation of emotions (Brien, 2012).

The national curriculum from Year 1 states that pupils should check that the text makes sense to them as they read and self-correct when what they have read does not fit in with their syntactic or semantic knowledge. These terms are summarised below.

Syntactic knowledge: this refers to the structure or grammatical correctness of a sentence such as word order.

Semantic knowledge: this refers to the meaning of the text and whether it makes sense to the reader based on their prior knowledge.

A sentence could be structurally or grammatically incorrect (syntax) but still have meaning. Many readers use their knowledge of syntax and semantic knowledge when reading to self-correct and to check that what they have read is accurate. The context in which the word in written (syntax and semantics) can give information about whether the word has been read accurately.

Children also need to look at the **graphical features** of text (word length, shape) to check their reading accuracy.

Using knowledge of syntax, semantics and graphical features, you can ask pupils the following questions when reading.

- *Does it sound right?*
- *Does it make sense?*
- *Does it look right?*

Children can self-correct their responses to a word if they have read it incorrectly and through accurate word recognition they will develop a better understanding of the text.

Critical questions

» *Should comprehension strategies be used for word recognition as described above?*

» *What are the advantages of using knowledge of syntax and semantics for word recognition?*

» *What are the disadvantages?*

» *Do skilled readers self-correct through knowledge of the context in which the word is written or is this an attribute of poor readers?*

Reading as a writer

Effective readers are able to *read as a writer*. As they read texts they are able to consider:

- why the author may have chosen to use certain vocabulary;
- why the author has added emphasis to certain words, for example through the use of capitalisation;
- why the author has used specific punctuation;
- how the author has used grammar at word, sentence or text level.

Understanding why the author has made certain decisions when composing a text will help children to think more clearly about the impact they are trying to make on the reader when they produce their own writing (*writing as a reader*). However, before children are able to write like this they need to consider how authors have used language to create effect as they read texts created by others. Both processes, reading as a writer and writing as a reader, are therefore connected, and effective readers will be able to discuss the choices that authors have made when constructing texts and the impact this creates on the reader.

Teaching children to read as a writer can be a focus during shared and guided reading sessions. When you plan these lessons you need to carefully consider the questions you are going to ask children to develop this level of comprehension.

* Can you spot any adjectives?

* Why do you think the author used adjectives to describe the setting for this story?

* How do these adjectives help you as a reader?

* Why do you think the author has used an exclamation mark at the end of that sentence?

* Why do you think the author decided to write that word in capital letters?

* Can you spot any adverbs?

* Why do you think the author has used adverbs? How do they help you as a reader?

* Why has the author used sub-headings in this text?

* Can you spot any pronouns in this text? Why do you think the author has used pronouns?

These questions can be extended as children's comprehension develops. Challenging questions could include the following:

* Why do you think the author has used subordination?

* Why has the author used expanded noun phrases?

* Why do you think the author has used a question?

The focus is on developing children's understanding of what impact the author is trying to create on the reader when they make decisions about choice of grammar, presentation or punctuation. Children will only have a partial understanding of a text unless they are able to put themselves in the shoes of the author and consider the relationship between the text and the reader.

Reading pictures

Long before pupils start to read the printed word, teachers can start to develop their comprehension skills through supporting them in 'reading' pictures. The purpose of this is to develop their comprehension of a picture through the use of guided questioning. You might ask questions such as:

* Where is this? *Focus on the setting.*

* What can you see in the picture? *Focus on the identification of nouns.*

- What is happening? What are they doing? *Focus on the event[s].*

- Why might this be happening? *Early stages of developing inference.*

You can begin this process by just using one picture. You can then extend this by presenting children with a series of pictures representing the setting, characters and events from a story. You can then ask the pupils to talk through the story with you orally.

As children then start to read books it is important to ask them to use the pictures to support their comprehension of the story. After they have read the text, you can then ask them questions about the pictures to support their understanding. Sometimes the pictures completely support the text. However, in some texts, the illustrations extend the story further. It is important that children know that the illustrations are important in supporting their understanding of the text. We do not advocate that children should use picture cues as a word recognition strategy, but we do support the use of illustrations to facilitate children's understanding of the text.

Developing familiarity with texts

Children's understanding of a text will improve as they become more familiar with it. In the EYFS and in Key Stage 1, children need to be provided with opportunities to develop their familiarity with texts. Developing familiarity with stories helps children to understand the sequence of events and the characters in the text. You need to use a range of activities to develop familiarity with stories.

Book introductions

Book introductions are important in terms of setting the context. It is common practice for teachers to spend time discussing aspects of the book such as the cover, title, name of the author, name of the illustrator, the blurb. It is good practice to 'walk through' the book with children before they read it. This will give the pupils an opportunity to look at the illustrations and gain a sense of the text. You can use this as an opportunity to draw children's attention to specific new vocabulary which is included in the text and to any structural or presentational features of the text. Spending time on these initial activities will make the tasks of word recognition and comprehension easier for children.

Building memory

Children need good memories to be able to recall the sequence of events in a story. You can support the development of children's memories through the use of some simple activities. *Kym's Game* is a traditional game which helps to train the memory. In it, pupils are presented with a set of objects on a tray. They are asked to look at these objects and remember them. The pupils then close their eyes and one item is removed. They are then asked to open their eyes and say what item is missing. You can make this game more or less complicated by increasing or decreasing the number of items on the tray or by removing more than one item.

Retelling stories

Early reading comprehension starts with children being able to retell a story. To support young children in this process they need to develop familiarity with some well-known stories and they need to hear them time and time again. Children love hearing a story several times and very often they have a favourite story which they like to hear several times. Familiarity with stories will help children when they come to retelling it. If they know a story really well then retelling it will not be too much of a challenge.

Some ways of developing familiarity with stories include:

*   listening to a story several times;
*   listening to a story using a range of digital media as well as text;
*   using puppets to re-enact stories they have heard;
*   making collages or paintings of characters from stories;
*   creating a role-play area which enables children to re-enact the story;
*   making masks of characters so that children can re-enact the story;
*   creating a story-teller's chair so that children can orally retell the story.

Sequencing events

To develop children's understanding of sequencing events from stories you can use a washing line. Colour photocopy and laminate some illustrations from the story. These could include an illustration of the setting, illustrations to show key events from the story and an illustration of the ending. The illustrations can be pegged onto the washing line and arranged in the wrong order. You can ask the pupils to help you to arrange the illustrations in the correct order to assess their understanding of the story. The number of events selected could be increased or reduced depending on the abilities of the children and you could position vocabulary in between the illustrations to develop children's understanding of time (*first, next, then, after that, finally*).

To maximise participation and to get a more accurate assessment of their sequencing skills you could get the children to work in pairs to do this activity without the aid of a washing line. You would simply provide them with smaller laminated illustrations and ask them to order them on a time line or a story map. Sequencing activities can also be carried out on the interactive whiteboard. Children are presented with the pictures or text of the story, depending on their abilities, and they can move these around into the correct positions on the board.

Making predictions

Asking children to make predictions about what might happen next in a story is an obvious way of assessing their understanding of the text they are reading or listening to. You can do this by reaching a specific point in a story and asking the children to talk through with a response partner what they think might happen next. When children become skilled in making oral predictions, you can ask them to write down predictions on sticky notes and use these as a focus for discussion.

Questioning

Asking questions about texts enables you to assess children's understanding and extend their thinking. Bloom's Taxonomy (Bloom, 1984) provides a useful hierarchical framework for planning higher-order questioning which promotes thinking. The stages of the model can help you to plan increasingly challenging questions to cater for the needs of more able learners. The examples below illustrate how the model could be applied to reading comprehension.

Knowledge: literal comprehension questions that require children to recall facts from texts (Who? What? Where? When? How?).

Comprehension: questions that require children to explain something by piecing together information which is in the text. The answers to these questions will not be directly stated in the text. Children will be expected to read between the lines to give a suitable response.

Application: What other examples of X are there in the text?

Analysis: Close reference to the text to substantiate something: what is the evidence for X in the text?

Synthesis: How could we improve this story?

Evaluation: What did you think about this story? What was your favourite part and why? How does this story compare to other stories?

Examples of questions could include:

* Who is the most important character in this story?

* What do we know about the setting?

* Why has the writer used this word or this punctuation?

* What do you see in your mind as you read this?

* What is the effect of the use of rhyme in this poem or story?

* How can we find the information quickly in this text?

* Why has the author used diagrams to support the text?

* What sort of character is X?

Encouraging children to ask their own questions about texts they read or listen to is a powerful way of getting them to engage closely with texts.

CASE STUDY

Children asking questions about texts

Sally is a trainee teacher working with a Year 2 class. She has read *The True Story of the Three Little Pigs* by Jon Scieszka, which the children have really enjoyed. Sally now wants the children to start to ask questions about the story. She asks them to work in pairs and she gives them some time to think through the questions they would like to ask the wolf. Using hot seating (see Chapter 11), Sally then takes on the role of the Wolf. The children asked a range of questions. These included:

- *Why did you not just go to the shop to buy some sugar?*

- *Why did you eat the pigs when you blew the houses down?*

- *Why did you not report the death of the first little pig to the police?*

- *Why did you decide to make a cake if you had a cold?*

- *Why did the first little pig die when his house collapsed and it was only made out of straw?*

- *Why didn't you die when the straw house fell in?*

- *Why did you manage to survive each time the pigs' houses fell in?*

Critical questions

» *Why is it important for children to ask their own questions about texts?*

» *Teachers often ask more questions than children. As a trainee teacher, how can you model the process of asking questions about texts to children?*

Other reading comprehension strategies

The following strategies may support you in developing children's understanding of texts.

- **Visualisation:** *What picture do you now have in your head about the giant in Jack and the Beanstalk? What picture do you have in your head of the forest in Red Riding Hood?*

- **Drawing:** *Draw a picture of the setting for this story now that you have listened to the author's description of it.*

- **Story maps:** Ask children to plan out the events of a story in sequence onto a story map.

- **Sequencing and rearranging:** Present children with a jumbled-up story and ask them to re-order it into the correct sequence. Present children with jumbled-up text for instructions, recounts or non-chronological reports and ask them to organise the text into the appropriate sequence or position. In the case of non-chronological reports, they will need to organise the various pieces of information under the correct sub-headings.

- **Summarising:** Read to a certain point in a text then stop and ask the children to summarise the text up to this point.

- **Drawing characters:** Present children with a large outline of a character from a story and ask them to write words on the outline to describe the character. On the inside of the outline they can be asked to write words to describe the character's personality and on the exterior of the outline they can be asked to write words to describe the character's appearance.

- **Text highlighting:** Ask pupils to go through a piece of text and highlight all the words and phrases which tell them something about a character or setting.

- **Character ranking:** Ask children to rank characters from the kindest to the meanest in a story.

- **Writing a blurb:** Ask children to write their own blurb for a story they have listened to. This will enable you to check that they have understood the story.

- **Solving problems:** Read a story but stop at a point where a character faces a problem or dilemma. Ask the children for suggestions for how this problem might be solved and pool ideas together. Stop at key points of the story and ask them to tell you what they would do if they were characters in the story.

- **Best bit:** Ask them to tell you which bit was the funniest/scariest/best/worst and why.

- **Building vocabulary:** Build banks of new words that children encounter in texts and display these along with synonyms.

- **Meet the author:** Ask the children to think of questions that they would like to ask the author about the text. You could become the author of the text and, using hot seating (see Chapter 11), the children could be encouraged to ask you questions about the text. Once this process has been modelled you could ask the children to take on the role of being the author.

Inference

Inferential comprehension refers to the ability to piece together pieces of given information in order to answer a question where the answer cannot be directly extracted from the text. It is similar to doing detective work in that it involves searching for clues in the text. Asking inferential questions is a higher form of questioning than literal questions where the answers are obvious in the text. It involves reading between the lines. The ability of pupils to make inferences on the basis of what is being said or done in a text is now an expectation of pupils from Year 1 in the national curriculum.

Developing inferential comprehension is a skill you will need to model to the children, particularly in Year 1. You will need to explain that the answers might not be in the text but that the clues are there to help them find them and to demonstrate how to combine several pieces of information in a text to make an inference. Once you have modelled being a reading detective by finding the clues and making inferences, you will then be able to support them in developing this skill through guided and individual reading sessions.

Learning poetry by heart

There is a significant focus in the national curriculum on children being able to recite poetry by heart, starting in Year 1. The benefits of this include the following.

- It helps to develop the memory.
- It develops children's linguistic skills.
- It allows children's to refine their presentational skills.
- It develops self-confidence.
- It produces a sense of achievement.

Poems with repetitive structures will be easier for pupils to recite. In Year 2, children need to be introduced to a wider repertoire of poems and they should be encouraged to perform these out loud. You might want to consider introducing a *poem of the week* which children can practise daily. This can be displayed in the classroom and also taken home for pupils to learn. You can also find suitable poetry that relates to the class topic or theme and pupils can use the structures used in published poetry to write their own poems.

Critical questions

» *Why do children need to learn poetry?*

» *What is the value of learning poetry by heart?*

Shared and guided reading

You can use shared and guided reading to develop children's comprehension skills. Shared reading usually involves the reading of a text which is shared with a class. Guided reading is carried out in smaller groups and focuses on teaching children developmentally appropriate reading skills and techniques at the level at which the children are currently working.

In shared and guided reading, the texts chosen should be slightly above the level that the children can read independently. In shared reading, you need to encourage the children to participate in the process. This could be through asking them to join in with parts of the text or through questioning them about the text. You will need to ask them a variety of closed questions which focus on developing literal understanding and open questions which develop their inferential, evaluative and appreciative comprehension.

In guided reading, there should be a clear focus to the session. You need to be very clear on what you want the children to learn. A guided reading session could be specifically planned to develop pupils' literal understanding, or with more able children, you might want to develop their inferential, evaluative and appreciative comprehension skills. You might want to focus on developing their skills in prediction or you might want to plan a lesson which focuses on developing understanding of reading with expression. Additionally, a lesson could be designed to focus on developing children's understanding of reading taking account of punctuation or you might want to focus on self-correcting using syntactic and semantic knowledge.

You will need to plan your questions carefully and you might want to revisit Bloom's Taxonomy to help you plan questions which are suitable for the group you are working with. In guided reading, you also need to make explicit reference to the pupils' prior learning in phonics and, again, this needs to be closely related to the level of phonics knowledge of the group you are working with. For example, if you have introduced a specific group of pupils to the split vowel digraph in their phonics lessons, you might then select a text which encourages them to apply this knowledge in their reading.

Critical questions

» *Have a look at some reading comprehension papers from the Key Stage 1 Statutory Assessment Tests. Look at the mark schemes. What types of questions are used on the tests to assess achievement in reading comprehension at different levels?*

» *Is it important for teachers to train children in how to complete reading comprehension test papers? What are the advantages and limitations of this?*

Critical points

» *Reading needs to be taught within the context of a language-rich environment.*

» *Reading comprehension ability is dependent upon a child's ability to decode words as well as their linguistic comprehension. Good ability in each of these domains is needed to support the development of good reading ability.*

» *Children who decode print well but do not understand it cannot be considered to be good readers.*

» *As children read more, their language comprehension skills improve because the task of reading introduces children to a wider range of vocabulary.*

Chapter reflections

This chapter has emphasised the importance of reading for understanding. The purpose of reading is essentially to gather meaning, and accurate decoding alone does not produce good readers. We have emphasised the importance of linguistic comprehension in laying the foundations for good reading comprehension. The teaching of reading should therefore be embedded within a broad and rich language curriculum in which children are immersed in rich spoken-language contexts. Once linguistic comprehension and accurate decoding are established, teachers can then focus more specifically on using strategies for developing reading comprehension. These have been summarised in this chapter.

Taking it further

The Primary National Strategies produced three booklets on reading comprehension which support many of the ideas in this chapter. They are well worth reading.

DfES (2005) *Understanding Reading Comprehension: 1: What is reading comprehension?* Nottingham: DfES.

DfES (2005) *Understanding Reading Comprehension: 2: Strategies to develop reading comprehension*. Nottingham: DfES.

DfES (2005) *Understanding Reading Comprehension: 3: Further strategies to develop reading comprehension*. Nottingham: DfES.

References

Bernstein, B (1971) *Class, Codes and Control, Vol. 1: Theoretical Studies Towards Sociology of Language*. London: Routledge & Kegan Paul.

Bloom, B (1984) *Taxonomy of Educational Objectives*. Boston, MA: Pearson.

Brien, J (2012) *Teaching Primary English*. London: Sage.

Bruce, T (2004) *Developing Learning in Early Childhood*. London: Paul Chapman.

Department for Education (DfE) (2013) *The National Curriculum in England: Key Stages 1 and 2 Framework Document*. London: DfE.

DfES (2004) *The Effective Provision of Pre-School Education (EPPE) Project: A Longitudinal Study Published by the DfES, 1997–2004*. Nottingham: DfES.

Gough, P B, and Tunmer, W E (1986) Decoding, Reading and Reading Disability. *Remedial Special Education*, 7: 6–10.

Hoover, W A, and Gough, P B (1990) The Simple View of Reading. *Reading and Writing*, 2: 127–60.

Johnston, R, and Watson, J (2007) *Teaching Synthetic Phonics*. Exeter: Learning Matters.

Lambirth, A (2006) Challenging the Laws of Talk: Ground Rules, Social Reproduction and the Curriculum. *The Curriculum Journal*, 17: 59–71.

Rose, J (2006) *Independent Review in the Teaching of Early Reading: Final Report*. Nottingham: DfES.

Vygotsky, L (1978) *Mind in Society*. Cambridge, MA: Harvard University Press.

6 Reading comprehension: Key Stage 2

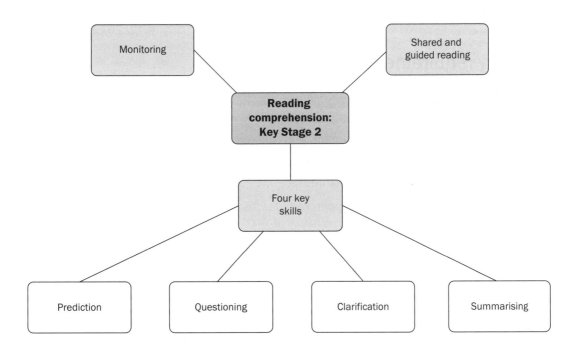

Teachers' Standards

TS3: Demonstrate good subject and curriculum knowledge

Trainees must:

* have a secure knowledge of the relevant subject(s) and curriculum areas, foster and maintain pupils' interest in the subject, and address misunderstandings.

National curriculum links

Reading comprehension

The national curriculum states that:

> *Pupils in Years 3 and 4 should be developing their understanding and enjoyment of stories, poetry, plays and non-fiction, and learning to read silently. They should be learning to justify their views about what they have read ... they should demonstrate understanding of figurative language, distinguish shades of meaning among related words and use age-appropriate academic language.*
>
> (DfE, 2013, p 33)

> *Pupils in Years 5 and 6 should be reading widely and frequently, for pleasure and information. They should be able to summarise and present a familiar story in their own words. They should be able to read silently and then discuss what they have read.*
>
> (DfE, 2013, p 41)

Statutory requirements

The statutory requirements for reading comprehension for pupils in Years 3–4 state that pupils should be taught to:

- *Develop positive attitudes to reading and understanding of what they read by:*
    - *listening to and discussing a wide range of fiction, poetry, plays, non-fiction and reference books or textbooks;*
    - *reading books that are structured in different ways and reading for a range of purposes;*
    - *using dictionaries to check the meaning of words that they have read;*
    - *increasing their familiarity with a wide range of books, including fairy stories, myths and legends, and retelling some of these orally;*
    - *identifying themes and conventions in a wide range of books;*
    - *preparing poems and play scripts to read aloud and to perform, showing understanding through intonation, tone, volume and action;*
    - *discussing words and phrases that capture the reader's interest and imagination;*
    - *recognising different forms of poetry.*
- *Understand what they read, in books they can read independently, by:*
    - *checking that the text makes sense to them, discussing their understanding and explaining the meaning of words in context;*

- – *asking questions to improve their understanding of a text;*
- – *drawing inferences such as inferring characters' feelings, thoughts and motives from their actions, and justifying inferences with evidence;*
- – *predicting what might happen from details stated and implied;*
- – *identifying main ideas drawn from more than one paragraph and summarising these;*
- – *identifying how language, structure, and presentation contribute to meaning.*
- • *retrieve and record information from non-fiction;*
- • *participate in discussion about both books that are read to them and those they can read for themselves, taking turns and listening to what others say.*

In Years 5–6, children should also be taught to:

- • *Maintain positive attitudes to reading and understanding of what they read by:*
  - – *increasing their familiarity with a wide range of books, including myths, legends and traditional stories, modern fiction, fiction from our literary heritage, and books from other cultures and traditions;*
  - – *recommending books that they have read to their peers, giving reasons for their choices;*
  - – *making comparisons within and across books;*
  - – *learning a wider range of poetry by heart preparing poems and play scripts to read aloud and to perform, showing understanding through intonation, tone, and volume so that the meaning is clear to an audience.*
- • *Understanding what they read by:*
  - – *summarising the main ideas drawn from more than one paragraph*
  - – *identifying key details that support the main ideas.*
- • *discuss and evaluate how authors use language, including figurative language, considering the impact on the reader;*
- • *retrieve, record and present information from non-fiction;*
- • *participate in discussion about both books that are read to them and those they can read for themselves, building on their own and others' ideas and challenging views courteously;*
- • *explain and discuss their understanding of what they have read, including through formal presentations and debates, maintaining a focus on the topic and using notes where necessary;*
- • *provide reasoned justification for their views.*

Introduction

By the beginning of Key Stage 2 there is a belief that the majority of children move from *learning to read* to *reading to learn*. Our education system dictates that most new learning is accessed through reading, so truly understanding those little black marks on a page becomes imperative. As we are introduced to new and more complicated texts we begin to realise that comprehension is a never-ending task of constructing meaning – a job for life. As teachers, you need to develop your pupils as active readers. Comprehension must be taught across all subjects and it must be taught explicitly. Like any other skill, it needs to be modelled and children need to know what good comprehenders do.

As you have seen, word recognition and language comprehension work in tandem to allow the reader to make meaning from the text being read. As children work towards independence and become active readers, they control their own cognitive processes and develop metacognitive skills to monitor their performance. This chapter will focus on the strategies that need to be taught to secure this independence and the importance of making meaning before, during and after reading. It will introduce you to a range of interactive activities that promote positive attitudes to reading for purpose and enjoyment. Motivating your children to want to read is a key responsibility in all your teaching, and they need to see you as a reader, a reader who enthusiastically absorbs the worlds and new knowledge that texts open up to you. Don't make it look simple, because it isn't. Let them see you work and explore different strategies to discover hidden meanings, savour rich vocabulary and question authors' intentions.

Reading is probably the hardest skill we ask our children to master, but it should also be the most rewarding.

Four key skills

In Key Stage 2 the children continue to ask themselves the key questions that allow them to orchestrate the three sources of information defined in Chapter 5.

1. Does it make sense? Semantic.

2. Does it sound right? Syntactic.

3. Does it look right? Visual/graphic.

If the answer to these questions is *'yes'* then the reader proceeds. If, however, the answer is *'no'* to any one of these questions then the reader needs to stop and select a strategy to address the problem. This may involve decoding, rereading or reading on to gauge context. The strategy they choose must be appropriate to the problem to be solved and they need to cross-check against the other two sources to continue.

They must also identify and further develop the four key skills that successful readers use whenever they are reading. These are the skills of **prediction**, **questioning**, **clarification** and **summarising**. These have been introduced in the previous chapter, but we will now consider them in more detail and explore how they too must be orchestrated together to achieve in-depth comprehension in reading.

Prediction

A prediction is what someone thinks will happen and, in the context of reading, it is based upon prior knowledge and evidence found in the text. It is a search for meaning before we even begin to read. The evidence may simply be the title and illustration on the front cover of a book. If we see the storybook being read is called *Lost* and the illustration shows a dark forest, it would be an acceptable prediction to suppose that someone is going to get lost in the forest. If we also have experiences of walking in large wooded areas we might also agree that getting lost is a real possibility. Our prediction relies on our knowing a meaning for the word *lost* and knowing what the illustration depicts. It also relies upon understanding that our own personal experience contributes to our comprehension of any text.

It is vital that children understand that while a prediction has to be sensible (if we predicted that the above text was going to be about a journey into space it might be questioned), it does not have to be correct. We can change our prediction at any time during and after reading as new information is offered. The above text was actually about a small community's losing battle to stop the construction of a large factory complex outside their village. Older children are often prepared to take fewer risks. They are less prepared to make predictions and are constrained by a fear of being wrong. It is the teacher's role to model that it doesn't matter if you are wrong initially so long as you reflect, review and correct as you read.

Prediction is not about knowing, and the language of prediction needs to be taught – *'I think'*, *'I imagine'*, *'I conclude'*; not *'I know'*. To be able to make sensible predictions, the reader needs to know where to look for clues. Text introductions don't become less important for older or more successful readers, particularly as the texts become more complicated both in structure and content. Are the clues in the layout, the diagrams, the chapter titles or the language used? In Key Stage 2, the children need to learn how to introduce a text to themselves if they are to become truly independent readers, and you will need to continue to model this until they are ready to take on that responsibility. As adults we introduce texts to ourselves and identify the clues to the genre and content – we pick up a book or a newspaper and skim to find the main idea or scan to locate a specific detail. These are skills that children need to develop as they move through school, particularly when working with non-fiction texts or making their own book choices.

Activities to support prediction

In Key Stage 2, as texts become longer and the reader needs to establish cohesion across chapters, prediction continues during and after reading, allowing the reader to make connections not only within one text but across several texts. This allows them to identify themes and conventions and recognise details that are both stated and implied. They begin to make comparisons within and across texts as they develop preferences and express opinions.

That reminds me!

These are sometimes referred to as 'double-entry journals' and can be used with an individual text or with a range of texts that share a common theme. Once modelled, the children can keep them independently and share them with a partner or in a group. Each page of the journal is split into two – on the left-hand side they note down a quote/key event/character/ setting, etc, and on the right-hand side they record what it reminds them of. This may be a similar character in another story or a historical reference that links a novel set in Victorian times to non-fiction text on childhood in the late 1800s. Making these connections allows the reader to predict what might happen in the text being read.

Words, words, words

Before reading an article or text, give the children some keywords. They should annotate the words and discuss with a partner what they think they have in common. They should make predictions about the themes and subject of the text based on the connotations of the words they have been given, eg medals, teamwork, torch, commitment = Olympics.

DRTA (directed reading thinking activity) (Jennings and Shepherd, 1998)

Reveal a text to the children in small sections. As each chunk is introduced, ask them to make predictions. They then reach conclusions as they read, supporting these ideas using evidence from the text.

1. The children make predictions about the text using the title.

2. The children read to a prescribed point.

3. They stop and review their predictions discussing:

   - what they know;

   - how they know;

   - what they think will happen next.

4. They read the next section and ask the same types of questions to either confirm or disprove their predictions.

5. The sequence continues with the children explaining and justifying their predictions.

Picture this

Working on their own, the children read a set section of a text. They then predict and draw what happens next using quotes from the text to support. They share their ideas with a partner and compare predictions and how they have supported them with evidence from the text. An alternative to this (which supports writing composition, see Chapter 10) has the children working in pairs to write a 'Carry On' story. Having read the set section of a fiction text, they each write their own version of the next part of the story. They then compare their composition and justify their choices based on evidence from the original text.

Before and after (using prior knowledge)

Before reading a non-fiction text, the children draw a simple spidergram showing what they know about the subject. This should include predictions of what they expect to find out from the text. After reading, they use a different colour to change misconceptions and add new knowledge to their diagram.

Critical question

»   *How do prediction skills in reading enrich composition skills in writing?*

Questioning

Good readers ask themselves questions before, during and after reading. These may be questions seeking information or clarification or questions that express doubt or disagreement. Successful readers interact with the text. Again, the skill of questioning must be modelled and, as explored in Chapter 5, this is first achieved by posing questions that require children to become 'detectives' to answer. Don't leave your questions about the text until after reading. Give the children a purpose to begin reading and set them a quest, whether that be selecting words and phrases that capture the reader's interest and imagination or identifying characters' feelings, thoughts and motives from their actions.

Understanding the purpose for reading is at the heart of engaging with a text and being able to truly comprehend what is read. As they become more independent in Key Stage 2, the children need to be able to evaluate the reading task they are undertaking. This is where the questioning begins and is very much linked to prediction. If you know the purpose then you can tell whether you are being successful. If you can identify the structure of the text then you begin to understand how information is organised and what kind of meaning you are searching for, whether that be literal, inferential or evaluative. Readers must ask themselves:

*   What is it about? (eg earthquakes)

*   What kind of reading is it? (explanation)

*   Why am I reading this? (to find out the causes of earthquakes)

*   How long will it take me to read? (can I skim and scan?)

As you can see, comprehension is as much about asking questions as it is about answering them. The more we generate our own 'wonderings' and then seek the answers, the more independent and successful we become as readers. The richest learning comes from answering our own questions. I am more likely to recognise a question about authorial intent if I can generate my own. To give this 'detective work' purpose it is important that these questions are directed towards a text that we have some ownership of or commitment to. Stand-alone comprehension exercises on random extracts may give some practice in answering specific question types, but it is more likely that the children will engage with a text they are currently reading, eg one being shared in a guided reading session. While we are developing our own questioning skills we need to have some prior knowledge of the text. As with all good teaching, you should start with the known – let the child generate questions around a familiar story first. They can then apply this skill to new and more complicated texts.

A Reminder: In the previous chapter we identified the three main types of comprehension questions: literal, inferential and evaluative.

1. **Literal**: the answer is right there in the text and can be 'lifted' directly from it.

2. **Inferential**: the answer requires the reader to read between the lines and make their own connections. As they infer they use deduction and interpretation.

3. **Evaluative**: the answer requires the reader to make a judgement or choice and justify these. This includes 'reading like a writer' and identifying the author's intentions regarding what they are trying to communicate and how they use structure and language to achieve it.

Consider the following text and examples of questions that might be asked:

> *Goldilocks arrived at the three bears' house as the sun rose over the hill. The door was unlocked and so she carefully lifted the latch and entered.*

- Literal question: Whose house was it? (the three bears')

- Inferential question: What time of day was it? (early morning)

- Evaluative question: Should Goldilocks have entered the house?

From an early age, children are able to answer these types of questions as they are guided by an 'expert other' (Vygotsky, 1978), but in Key Stage 2 we are again focusing on independence and so the children need frequent opportunities to practise and hone their questioning skills. The following activities not only give them these opportunities, but also give you as the teacher the possibility for ongoing assessment.

Activities to support literal questioning

Sequencing text

We looked at sequencing illustrations in Key Stage 1 to consolidate the children's literal understanding of the key events in a story or non-fiction process such as the life cycle of a frog. This activity can be developed throughout Key Stage 2 using text, beginning with key sentences and leading into paragraphs or key extracts from chapters. The focus is on identifying cohesion, whether through chronological order or character development. The text might be fiction, where the children are showing their literal understanding of the key structure, eg plot development through introduction to character/setting through problem to resolution to ending. Or it may be exploration of autobiography, where attention would focus on identifying key dates.

Question jigsaw

The children are given a simple 'jigsaw' template with four to six segments. On each is written a key question: When? Who? Where? What? The children might begin by generating very simple literal questions related to the text as a whole, eg *When did this story take place? Where is the story set? Who are the main characters? What was the main event?* They then work either individually or with a partner to answer their own questions with reference to the text, collecting evidence and lifting their answers directly from the text itself. These questions can become much more specific and focus directly on a character's development, eg *When do we first meet Character X? Where do they travel to? Who do they meet? What do they find?* The 'jigsaw' becomes larger and might introduce inferential questions when they add the key questions how and why.

Wanted poster

The children create a wanted poster for a specific character. They both draw the character and write a clear description, retrieving phrases directly from the text to support their understanding of the information given. To begin with, this may be simply appearance, but it can be extended to explore personality traits and key actions.

Question and answer speech bubbles

Working with a partner, the children write their own literal questions about events/characters/investigations in science on a speech bubble which they swap with their partner. Their partner then writes the answer to the question on another speech bubble and they share their dialogue. This can be done with small speech-bubble sticky notes and stuck onto a large outline or illustration of the character.

Activities to support inferential questioning

Thought bubbles

As above, but now the focus is on what you are inferring or deducing from the text. Again, evidence should be retrieved from the text, perhaps using page numbers so that references can be explored during the dialogue.

Axis of emotion

A simple grid with an x and y axis is needed for this. On the vertical axis might be three faces, one above the other, sadness, contentment and happiness (the emotions are changed according to the focus, eg fear, confusion), while on the horizontal axis are recorded key moments in the story. The children plot the changing emotions of the character during the story, eg Cinderella moving between extremes of unhappiness and joy. They begin to make inferences around cause and effect. Another character can be added to explore the relationships between characters and how they interact and affect each other, eg if we add an ugly sister we can see that there is a direct link showing opposite emotions at any given time during the story.

Matching game

The children are given two sets of cards. On one set are phrases or extracts from the text and on the other are inference words or statements:

    'The leaves were red, orange and yellow' → autumn
    'The boy dabbed his eyes with the tissue' → upset

This can also be linked to figurative speech, which is something that many children struggle to understand. While it is impossible to introduce children to all examples of this, they do need to explore that words don't always mean what they literally say, eg

'The team were on fire' → The team were playing extremely well

'The house was a handyman's dream' → The house was falling to pieces

Activities to support evaluative questioning

Axis of emotion

As above, but now the children are plotting their own responses to a text. They might be recording how their own feelings change during the course of the text or where their sympathies might be at any given time.

Language detective

The children are given a grid. In the left-hand column they record words and phrases (about characters/settings/actions) that the author uses, and in the right-hand column they record the impact the word choice has on them as a reader. Many children find it difficult to express their responses to language and authorial intent, so it is important that you model the language of response and offer speaking and writing frames to help them, eg *The author creates tension by using words like... /I think the author wants me to feel... because...*

Critical question

» *Why is it imperative that you know and have read the texts that the children are reading?*

Clarification

When we clarify something we aim to make it less confused and so more easily understandable. To be able to clarify we must first identify that we don't fully understand. This may be a word, a phrase or a whole concept. While some children don't realise they have misunderstood, others are fearful of admitting it. As adults we are often guilty of this ourselves – we don't want to appear foolish in front of our peers. Children are no different, especially as they grow older. However, if they accept that they don't understand what they are reading and carry on regardless, their overall comprehension will be poor. For this reason, it is vital that you make it clear that it is all right not to understand and that many good readers have to clarify parts of a text. Indeed, it is this identification of a loss of meaning that makes them good readers; it is only foolish when we don't understand and do nothing about it. To begin with, children look to you to clarify for them, and through careful text introductions, you will often be able to do this before they even begin to read. (Look again at the critical question above.) However, as they become more independent they must do this for themselves.

CASE STUDY

Amar

Amar was working with a group of Year 4 children, all of whom were second-language users, as they read a story about a dog that lived with a family on a canal boat. The concept and language of narrow boats and locks had been new to the children and a lot of pre-reading work had been undertaken to prepare them for the 'technical' language they would encounter. However, it was unpredictable 'tricky' words that caused the problems and needed clarifying. As he read with one child, a boy who was reading with some fluency, came to the word *tug* and stopped – the sentence was about a member of the family fishing when *'he felt a small tug on the line'*. The child sounded and blended successfully but again stopped and tried a different strategy as he reread from the beginning of the sentence – again he stopped. This child had recognised that meaning had been lost and needed clarifying and, having tried the strategies he knew, turned to Amar for help. At first Amar was confused as this was a word that the child could decode easily, but it soon became clear that it was an *'old word in a new context'*. The boy only new one meaning of the word *tug* and could not work out what a small boat was doing on the end of a fishing line.

Another child could be heard reading *'it was hot and the dog sat on the towpath painting'*. This child did not question what she had read and continued. When Amar questioned her it became clear that she did not know the word *panting* and so had substituted a known word without questioning whether it made sense. The teacher demonstrated the meaning of *panting*, and at the end of the session when another child asked for *panting* to be clarified, he encouraged the first girl to demonstrate and define its meaning.

Critical questions

»   *Why did Amar ask the child to clarify the meaning of panting?*

»   *Is it important for children to see each other as sources of information?*

»   *Can an over-reliance on phonics sometimes hinder comprehension?*

The case study shows how understanding context is crucial to comprehension. Whether with new vocabulary or 'old' words with different meanings (homonyms), it is vital that children have strategies to clarify their usage. For this reason you need to offer plenty of opportunities for them to investigate and identify multiple definitions of words and place them into the context of meaningful sentences. They need to be able to use dictionaries to check the meanings of words and discover new definitions. Too often, children equate dictionaries only with spelling rather than as a tool to understand the words that they read.

Summarising

Being able to see the big picture is a vital comprehension skill. Summarising is all about tracking down the main idea in a text and then being able to express it both verbally and in writing. This is not a skill that children find easy and you will have to give them plenty of opportunities to use their own words to shorten a piece of text so that they include only the essential information. If we were to ask you what the main idea in *Goldilocks and the Three Bears* was, how would you answer? Children will go into detail about porridge and broken chairs, but, in reality, it is ultimately a tale about a young girl who breaks into a house and is caught in the act.

Critical question

» *Can you identify the main idea in other traditional tales such as Cinderella or Little Red Riding Hood?*

Of course, the aim of summarising doesn't immediately focus on a whole text, and to begin with, you will need to model and focus this skill on smaller chunks of text. When children are first introduced to chapter books the problem of coherence comes into focus and they are often unable to carry information from one chapter to another. It is important that, before moving on, they learn to summarise the important points introduced in the chapter and use this to predict what they think will happen next. In non-fiction text, where information is often presented in a number of forms, including diagrams and charts, they again need to be able to read these and not only summarise the key information but also link the various sources together to form an overall big picture. Again, it is crucial that you model the language of summarising, eg *'The most important idea/point in this chapter is... The boxes on this page show us...*

Activities to support summarising

Words, words, words

This is the reversal of the game used to support prediction. Now it is the children who must collect the keywords to summarise the text they have read. Working in pairs, they challenge another pair (who have not read the text) to identify its theme. Alternatively, they could work with a pair who have read the same text and produced their own keywords – where are they the same or different? They can swap words to produce a definitive set.

Story sticks

The children identify the key events in a story/chapter and record them on sticky notes (these may be illustrations or text), which they attach in sequence to a pea-stick. They then use them to retell the events in as few words as possible. (These can also be used to plan writing activities – either for retellings of familiar stories or for generating new ideas.)

Summary web

This is particularly useful for non-fiction, where chronological order is not necessarily import-ant. The children sit in a circle with one member of the group holding a ball of yarn. The first child states a key fact/point from the text and then throws the yarn across the circle to another child, who adds another key fact/point and throws the ball across the circle again.

This continues until a 'web' has been created of all the important facts that summarise the text.

Monitoring

To be independent readers children have to take responsibility for monitoring their own comprehension. They have to orchestrate all the skills explored in this chapter and respond to any loss of meaning. The new curriculum emphasises the importance of reading aloud and focuses attention on performing poetry (see Chapter 2 for a detailed examination of poetry, discussion and debate), but reading aloud is a key strategy for monitoring comprehension across all reading. While silent reading is a goal to be achieved throughout Key Stage 2, children should not be discouraged from reading aloud, particularly when tackling more complicated texts. It is when we read aloud to ourselves, a partner or a larger group that we can really identify through fluency and phrasing whether we have control of the text as a reader.

Shared and guided reading

These two teacher-led strategies were introduced in the previous chapter and are where the skills related to successful reading, both word reading and comprehension, are modelled and taught. In shared reading the teacher models the thinking behind these strategies and invites the children to engage with them and begin to practise these skills. In guided reading the teacher focuses on specific strategies and skills and begins to hand over the mantle of independent reading to their pupils. It is through this transference of responsibility that the teacher builds in the children the *'capacity to work as independent enquirers and creative thinkers'* (Cremin, 2009, p 8). It is during guided reading sessions that the activities introduced in this chapter should be modelled and taught to the groups.

Although it is only truly guided reading when an adult is working with the group, the aim continues to be that the children apply the skills and knowledge taught during these sessions to their independent reading, and many of the activities can be undertaken by the children when they are working in unsupported groups to both prepare them for new texts and assess their comprehension of familiar texts. This application can be taken a stage further through *'reciprocal reading'* sessions (Palincsar and Brown, 1986), which ultimately allow a group to work independently using all the strategies that would be present during a guided reading session. The children take on specific roles: the Leader, the Predictor, the Clarifier, the Summariser, the Questioner. They work together to interrogate and master a new text and in doing so instil the skills that they can call on when working alone.

Breaking down barriers

It is important that you are constantly assessing the barriers that may be preventing your pupils from becoming independent readers and these are most apparent when working with a guided reading group. Although all children are individuals and their strengths and weaknesses should not be generalised, some generic issues need to be addressed. These relate to reading stamina, a lack of independent strategies (or rather the specific knowledge of what they have control of, ie using the appropriate strategies), limited vocabulary, coherence across a text and failing to see each other as sources of information. All of these barriers need to be explored, and what might be called 'the Four Rs' is a useful mantra to share with the children: **Revisit** strategies regularly, **Remind** the children what they have control of, **Reduce** the amount of text being read so that they can practise their skills, and constantly offer opportunities for specific **Retrieval** of evidence from a broad range of texts.

Finally, don't flit from one text type to another, particularly with less-confident readers. Although they must read a broad range of texts, give them plenty of practise on each. If in Lower Key Stage 2 they have been introduced to their first chapter book and all the challenges it presents, then let the next book also be a chapter book so that they can practise and apply their new-found skills.

Critical points

» *Word reading and language comprehension work in tandem to construct meaning.*

» *The task of constructing meaning is 'a job for life'.*

» *Comprehension is as much about asking questions as about answering them.*

» *Comprehension skills must be explicitly taught and modelled. Always start with the known and call upon prior knowledge and experience to support understanding.*

» *Skills and strategies for comprehension should be modelled and taught during shared and guided reading sessions.*

Chapter reflections

This chapter has focused on the four key comprehension skills of prediction, questioning, clarification and summarising. These must be orchestrated together and with growing independence if a child is to become an active and successful reader. We can only be truly classified as readers if we understand and can discuss the texts we read, justifying our opinions and statements by drawing evidence from the text and continue to generate questions. These skills and strategies must be taught through interactive experiences that both motivate children and instil in them a positive attitude towards reading. It is your goal to make reading a joyful experience that opens up new worlds to the children in your care – it should never be a chore.

Taking it further

Cameron, S (2009) *Teaching Reading Comprehension Strategies: A Practical Classroom Guide*. New Zealand: Pearson Education.

Cameron, S (2009) *The Reading Activity Handbook*. New Zealand: Pearson Education.

Davis, A (2011) *Building Comprehension Strategies: For the Primary Years*. Australia: Eleanor Curtain Publishing.

Oczjus, L D (2010) *Reciprocal Teaching at Work*. Newark, DE: International Reading Association.

References

Cremin, T (2009) *Teaching English Creatively*. London: Routledge.

Department for Education (DfE) (2013) *The National Curriculum in England: Key Stages 1 and 2 Framework Document*. London: DfE.

Jennings, C, and Shepherd, J (1998) *Literacy and the Key Learning Areas: Successful Classroom Strategies*. Australia: Eleanor Curtain Publishing.

Palincsar, A S, and Brown, A L (1986) Interactive Teaching to Promote Independent Learning from Text. *The Reading Teacher*, 39(8): 771–77.

Vygotsky, L (1978) *Mind in Society*. Cambridge, MA: Harvard University Press.

7 Writing: transcription – Key Stage 1

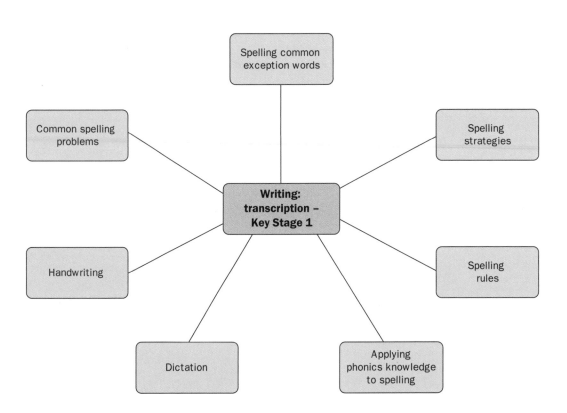

Spelling common exception words

Common spelling problems

Spelling strategies

Writing: transcription – Key Stage 1

Handwriting

Spelling rules

Dictation

Applying phonics knowledge to spelling

Teachers' Standards

TS3: Demonstrate good subject and curriculum knowledge

Trainees must:

*   have a secure knowledge of the relevant subject(s) and curriculum areas, foster and maintain pupils' interest in the subject, and address misunderstandings.

National curriculum links

Writing: transcription

The national curriculum states that:

> *Writing down ideas fluently depends on effective transcription: that is, on spelling quickly and accurately through knowing the relationship between sounds and letters (phonics) and understanding the morphology (word structure) and orthography (spelling structure) of words.*

> (DfE, 2013, p 15)

For pupils in Year 1 the national curriculum states that:

> *Pupils' writing during year 1 will generally develop at a slower pace than their reading. This is because they need to encode the sounds they hear in words (spelling skills), develop the physical skill needed for handwriting, and learn how to organise their ideas in writing.*

> (DfE, 2013, p 19)

The additional complexities of transcription in Year 2 are highlighted:

> *It is important to recognise that pupils begin to meet extra challenges in terms of spelling during year 2. Increasingly, they should learn that there is not always an obvious connection between the way a word is said and the way it is spelt. Variations include different ways of spelling the same sound, the use of so-called silent letters and groups of letters in some words and, sometimes, spelling that has become separated from the way that words are now pronounced, such as the 'le' ending in table. Pupils' motor skills also need to be sufficiently advanced for them to write down ideas that they may be able to compose orally. In addition, writing is intrinsically harder than reading: pupils are likely to be able to read and understand more complex writing (in terms of its vocabulary and structure) than they are capable of producing themselves.*

> (DfE, 2013, p 26)

Statutory requirements for Year 1

Spelling

Pupils should be taught to:

- spell:
  - words containing each of the 40+ phonemes already taught;
  - common exception words;
  - the days of the week.
- name the letters of the alphabet:
  - naming the letters of the alphabet in order;
  - using letter names to distinguish between alternative spellings of the same sound.
- add prefixes and suffixes:
  - using the spelling rule for adding –s or –es as the plural marker for nouns and the third person singular marker for verbs;
  - using the prefix un-;
  - using –ing, –ed, –er and –est *where no change is needed in the spelling of root words (eg* helping, helped, helper, quicker, quickest*)*.
- apply simple spelling rules and guidance, as listed in English Appendix 1 in the national curriculum;
- write from memory simple sentences dictated by the teacher that include words using the grapheme–phoneme correspondences and common exception words taught so far.

(DfE, 2013, p 22–23)

Handwriting

Pupils should be taught to:

- sit correctly at a table, holding a pencil comfortably and correctly;
- begin to form lower-case letters in the correct direction, starting and finishing in the right place;
- form capital letters;
- form digits 0–9;
- understand which letters belong to which handwriting 'families' (ie letters that are formed in similar ways), and practise these.

(DfE, 2013, p 24)

Statutory requirements for Year 2

Spelling

Pupils should be taught to:

- spell by:
    - segmenting spoken words into phonemes and representing these by graphemes, spelling many correctly;
    - learning new ways of spelling phonemes for which one or more spellings are already known, and learn some words with each spelling, including a few common homophones;
    - learning to spell common exception words;
    - learning to spell more words with contracted forms;
    - learning the possessive apostrophe (singular) [eg, the girl's book];
    - distinguishing between homophones and near homophones.
- add suffixes to spell longer words, including –ment, –ness, –ful, –less, –ly;
- apply spelling rules and guidance, as listed in English Appendix 1 of the national curriculum;
- write from memory simple sentences dictated by the teacher that include words using the GPCs, common exception words and punctuation taught so far.

(DfE, 2013, p 29–30)

Handwriting

Pupils should be taught to:

- form lower-case letters of the correct size relative to one another;
- start using some of the diagonal and horizontal strokes needed to join letters;
- understand which letters, when adjacent to one another, are best left unjoined;
- write capital letters and digits of the correct size, orientation and relationship to one another and to lower-case letters;
- use spacing between words that reflects the size of the letters.

(DfE, 2013, p 30)

Introduction

The ability to spell accurately is one of the indicators of a literate member of society. Primary teachers have a responsibility to ensure that all pupils can spell accurately by the time they leave primary school. Pupils who cannot spell in secondary schools are immediately disadvantaged because lack of automaticity in spelling slows down the writing process. Poor spelling can also lead to the development of a poor self-concept and this can impact achievement across the curriculum. We believe that with access to good teaching every child can learn to spell, regardless of socio-economic background, gender, ethnicity or special educational needs and/or disabilities. This chapter will provide you with some useful ideas for teaching spelling, although it is important to emphasise that different approaches work for different children.

The ability to produce neat, legible handwriting is important because children need to take pride in their work. Teachers play a crucial role in this respect by modelling neat, legible handwriting when writing on the board, in children's books and when making classroom labels. This chapter provides some useful strategies for developing pupils' handwriting.

Applying phonics knowledge to spelling

The national curriculum (DfE, 2013) states that children must be taught to read through the use of a systematic phonics programme. Through a systematic approach pupils will learn the sounds (phonemes) made by single letters, digraphs and trigraphs and they will be introduced to the complex alphabetic code. Pupils will use their phonic knowledge to read words (blending) by enunciating the sounds that the graphemes make within a word, saying these in sequence all the way through a word and combining them to read the target word. Pupils also need to use their phonic knowledge for spelling. This process is called segmenting or encoding. During the process of encoding, pupils hear each of the separate sounds (phonemes) within a spoken word and then they select or write the appropriate symbols to represent these sounds. The processes are reversible and should be taught consecutively within phonics lessons. The use of a *phoneme frame* may initially support pupils to segment words. In a phoneme frame pupils write each grapheme in a separate box as shown:

d	o	g

g	oa	t

l	igh	t

f	l	a	g

This will act as a scaffold by helping children to focus on the number of sounds they can hear within a word. The process can be broken down as follows.

- Listen to the spoken word.

- Use your fingers to count the phonemes you can hear in the word.

- Which phoneme can you hear first? Write down/select the grapheme that represents this phoneme.

- Which phoneme can you hear next? Write down/select the grapheme that represents this phoneme.

- Repeat the above process until you have written down or selected all of the graphemes that represent each phoneme in the word.

Initially, it is important to give the pupils words to spell which are within the scope of their existing phonic knowledge. For example, you would not ask pupils to spell the word *boil* if you have not taught the /oi/ grapheme–phoneme correspondence. Once pupils have applied their phonic knowledge to spell a word several times, the physical act of practising the spelling will mean that the spelling becomes more automatic and they may soon be able to spell it without hearing the sounds in the words. However, some pupils take longer to reach the stage of spelling words automatically and a multi-sensory approach might be necessary. To make your spelling lessons more memorable you could consider using the following approaches. You should be able to add your own ideas to this list:

- writing words in different-coloured sand;

- writing words in glitter;

- writing words in salt;

- writing words in cornflour mix;

- building words on magnetic boards using magnetic letters;

- using chunky chalks in the playground to write words on the ground;

- asking pupils to trace over each letter of a word where each letter has been made out of sandpaper;

- asking them to close their eyes visualise the word and to tell you the letters that they can see;

- writing words on slate boards using chalk;

- printing words using foam letters and paints;

- stamping letters out of malleable media (such as play-dough) to make words;

- using water pistols to write words outside on the floor;

- asking pupils to write words on paper using white wax crayons and getting them to paint over the page to reveal the word they have written.

Multi-sensory approaches to teaching spelling work effectively for all children. However, it is important that the process of segmenting words into their constituent sounds and representing these as graphemes is reinforced in all writing that children do, not just the writing they produce in the phonics lesson. When you model writing in front of the whole class (shared writing) ask the pupils to help you to segment words which are phonically regular. Reinforce the process of segmentation during guided writing and encourage pupils to apply this skill during their independent writing. Reading should be taught alongside spelling, and pupils need to understand that they can read back the words they have spelt. Pupils will start to spell many words in a phonetically plausible way once they master the skill of segmenting. You need to praise them for their attempts even when they spell an exception word using their phonic knowledge (eg they might spell *said* as *sed*). You should accept this until you have taught them the correct spelling. After this point, you should correct misspellings.

Spelling rules

The national curriculum (DfE, 2013) includes statutory rules and guidance to support the teaching of spelling and this is set out in Appendix 1 in the English strand of the primary national curriculum. Children can generally read more words than they can spell. Once they have been introduced to the alternative spellings of the graphemes in the complex alphabetic code, children need to make decisions about which graphemes to use in words (eg whether to write *leaf* or *leef*). Those children with a good memory may be able to remember which graphemes to use, and as children's reading develops, they will absorb the spellings of words less consciously through their reading. A multi-sensory approach to spelling, as described above, will help children to remember which graphemes to use in words because in this approach the correct spelling is reinforced visually, auditorily and kinaesthetically.

You need to teach the spelling rules explicitly and we recommend the following approach:

Revisit: revisit specific spelling rules that children have previously been taught, for example by focusing on those rules which the pupils find tricky.

Teach: Introduce the new rule by modelling how the rule works. You might want to show how the rule is applied to two or three words.

Practise: Give the children time to investigate the spelling rule, perhaps by organising them into pairs and asking them to apply the rule to other words. You might want them to find exceptions to the rule.

Apply: Give the children a sentence to write which requires them to apply the rule.

You need to bear in mind that just because children have been taught a rule does not mean that they will automatically apply that rule in their own independent writing. Children may be able to apply the rule within the spelling lesson but they may forget the rule when it comes to their own writing. If the children have been taught a rule you should make a specific point about this when you provide them with feedback, perhaps by reminding them of the rule and then giving them further opportunities to apply the rule.

(Glazzard and Stokoe, 2013)

Spelling strategies

Spelling by analogy

Teaching children to spell words by analogy can sometimes be useful. This strategy draws on children's knowledge of rime. For example, if pupils can spell *goat* because they recognise the rime /oat/ they are likely to be able to spell *coat* and even *throat*, but this strategy will not work for spelling *note*.

Critical question

» *Spelling words by analogy does not fit with a systematic synthetic phonics approach to spelling (described above) in which words are broken down into the smallest units of sound. However, we do not believe that one strategy works for all pupils. Do you agree with us?*

Mnemonics

These provide a way of spelling more difficult words such as:

* *necessary* – one collar and two sleeves;

* *because* – big elephants can always understand small elephants;

* *separate* – there is *a rat* in sep**arat**e;

* *said* – Sally-Anne is dancing.

(Glazzard and Stokoe, 2013)

Dictionaries

Dictionaries are a useful resource to support children with their independent writing. Learning to look up spellings or definitions of words breaks their dependency on you.

Start with simple picture dictionaries, but as the children progress beyond this you will need to teach them explicitly how dictionaries work. Show them how to find words in a dictionary using their knowledge of alphabetic ordering, first using the first letter only and then progressing to ordering words by their second and third letters. So that they can gain experience in ordering, give them words beginning with the same initial letter but with different subsequent letters and ask them to put the words in order. They also need experience of locating words in dictionaries. They need to be taught these skills in the daily literacy lesson and then they need opportunities to apply these skills when they are writing independently. The transference of this skill may not be automatic so you will need to reinforce it further in guided reading sessions. Children should also be taught how to use electronic dictionaries and simple electronic spell-checkers. Alphabet mats on tables to show alphabetic order are also useful (Glazzard and Stokoe, 2013, p 118).

Critical questions

» *Given the growth of technological hardware and software such as spell-checkers and electronic dictionaries, how important is it that children learn to spell?*

» *Should teachers correct all spelling mistakes in pupils' work?*

» *How can trainees with dyslexia benefit the teaching profession?*

Spelling through syllables

Words such as *pocket*, *rabbit*, *carrot* and *thunder* each have two syllables. You can teach pupils to clap the syllables and to use their phonic knowledge to spell each syllable in turn. They can then combine the spellings of the syllables to make the whole word.

Prefixes and suffixes

The prefixes and suffixes that pupils must be taught are identified in Appendix 1 of the national curriculum. These should be displayed in the classroom along with their root words. You can model the correct spelling by representing the prefix (or suffix) and root word in different colours.

Look, cover, write, check

This approach relies on a strong visual memory. The process works in the following way:

Look: children look at the word carefully, memorise it and say it.

Cover: children cover the word.

Write: children write the word from memory.

Check: children check their spelling attempt against the word.

Critical questions

»   *What are the advantages and disadvantages of this approach?*

»   *What are the arguments for and against spelling tests?*

»   *Do you agree that teachers should accept phonically plausible attempts at spelling?*

»   *Should teachers display children's work if there are spelling errors in it?*

»   *Should children in Year 1 and Year 2 be asked to redraft their writing so that the spelling is accurate? What are the arguments for and against this?*

»   *Why do pupils with dyslexia struggle with spelling? Research this.*

»   *How can teachers support pupils with dyslexia to improve their spelling? Research this.*

Spelling common exception words

Children will be introduced to exception words as part of their systematic phonics programme and they will be expected to learn to read and spell these words. The stage a pupil has reached within a phonics programme may determine whether a word is classed as an exception word or not. For example, in the very early stages of a phonics programme, the word *light* may be classed as an exception word. However, later in the programme, pupils will be introduced to the grapheme–phoneme correspondence /igh/ and this word is then phonically decodable. Some words are not phonically regular (eg *the, people, said*). These words cannot be spelt effectively using a phonics approach. You can teach the spellings of these words using approaches such as look, say, cover, write, check or mnemonics, although pupils may be able to use their phonic knowledge to spell the parts of the word which are phonically regular. These exception words should be displayed in the classroom on word walls, word banks or on word mats for pupils to access independently. Examples of common exception words that pupils need to be taught are listed in Appendix 1 of the national curriculum in England Key Stages 1 and 2 framework document (Reference: DfE-00178-2013).

CASE STUDY

Rupert: a trainee teacher with dyslexia

Rupert was a trainee teacher on a one-year postgraduate programme. He had a diagnosis of dyslexia but was unsure whether or not to declare this to his placement school. He could read well but found spelling particularly difficult. He discussed this with his training provider and his personal tutor agreed to set up a meeting with himself, Rupert and his school-based mentor. The mentor was very supportive and agreed to provide Rupert with a pocket-sized electronic spell-checker which Rupert could easily use during lessons if he needed help with spelling. It was agreed for Rupert to open up a discussion about dyslexia with his class, drawing on personal experiences, particularly in relation to strategies Rupert had found useful to support him with spelling. The training provider gave Rupert support with a recording device to enable him to record meetings and discussions with his mentors and the mentor agreed to provide Rupert with a weekly list of actions that needed to be completed by him.

Common spelling problems

Homophones and near homophones

A homophone is a word which has the same pronunciation as another word but has a different meaning and may differ in spelling. Examples include: *be/bee, blue/blew, sun/son, there/their/they're, hear/here, night/knight, see/sea, bare/bear*. Pupils need to be taught the difference in meaning between the different homophones.

Near homophones have a very similar pronunciation, for example, *quiet/quite* or *one/won*.

Critical question

» *How you how could teach homophones in an inspiring way?*

Contractions

In contractions (shortened forms), the apostrophe is placed where a letter or letters are omitted. Examples include *can't* (*cannot*), *didn't* (*did not*) and *I'll* (*I will*). Care should be taken with *its* and *it's*: *it's* is a contraction of *it is* (eg **It is** snowing [*It's snowing*], **It has** been snowing [*It's been snowing*]), and *its* is the possessive form. It's is never used for the possessive.

Critical question

» *Should children be taught to use contractions in their writing given that students in universities are normally not allowed to use them in academic writing?*

Possessive apostrophe

Pupils in Year 2 need to be taught the rules about apostrophe use for singular nouns. In the case of singular nouns, the apostrophe is placed before the 's'. For example, *the girl's pencil case, the boy's shoe.* This will need to be taught explicitly and should be reinforced through:

- shared and guided reading;
- marking and feedback on children's work;
- specific lessons;
- highlighting possessive apostrophes in texts;
- sorting apostrophe use on words into correct and incorrect use.

Dictation

Regular dictation will improve the practice children get with spelling and handwriting. Daily dictation will also improve children's confidence. We suggest that you choose sentences or captions that are within the scope of children's existing phonic knowledge. You can also include exception words that children have been taught. Once you have dictated the sentence and given the children time to write it, show them the correct model so that they can self-assess their writing. Ask the children to record their attempts using a range of materials, such as crayons, chalks or on small whiteboards with marker pens.

Critical question

» *What are the arguments for and against dictation?*

Handwriting

The following section is taken directly from Glazzard and Stokoe (2013).

Fine motor skills

Children need to have good manipulative skills, hand/eye co-ordination and finger strength in order to succeed in handwriting.

Manipulative skills can be developed using a range of resources. Play-dough is a very useful resource for this purpose and children can use it in a range of ways including squeezing, stretching, rolling and pressing. Finger puppets are also another valuable resource to help children manipulate their fingers. Using finger puppets children can separate their fingers wide apart, interlock their fingers, wiggle their fingers and thumb and open their fingers out from a fist one at a time.

Hand/eye co-ordination can be developed through:

- threading;
- using peg boards;
- weaving;
- using scissors;
- throwing and catching;
- hammering.

Finger/hand strength can be developed through:

- crushing paper;
- cutting thick card;
- squeezing a soft ball;
- digging;
- cutting food.

Unless these fine motor skills are developed first, children will find handwriting even more difficult because they will lack the foundations which are needed to control a writing implement.

Multi-sensory approaches

Children initially must master the hand movements necessary to form each letter. Initially these may be gross motor movements, and with practice children should then be encouraged to refine these same movements. When teaching letter formation the following steps will support you:

- **Look:** the teacher models the formation of a large letter on the board. Interactive white boards are not ideal for this purpose as the alignment is often inaccurate.
- **Trace:** the child traces over the letter repeatedly while also articulating the sound. Avoid tracing over dotted letters as children may focus on joining the dots and this will impede the flow of the letter formation.
- **Copy:** the child copies the letter repeatedly while also articulating the sound.
- **Write from memory:** the model is removed and the child practises the formation of the letter.
- **Eyes shut:** the child writes the letter from memory with their eyes shut to commit the letter formation to memory.

Letter formation should be practised using a variety of materials, including tracing in salt, sand and glitter, writing in the air, writing on each other's backs, tracing on hessian and silk or writing with water. It may be necessary to manipulate the child's hand to support letter formation. Initially the focus is on the child developing the correct movement for forming each letter. As the child progresses they can be introduced to tram lines which will help them to focus on proportion, ascenders and descenders.

Critical questions

» *When should children be introduced to writing in pen?*

» *How important is handwriting practice?*

» *How can teachers monitor letter formation?*

» *When children are writing freely would you continue to insist upon correct letter formation? How would you support your argument?*

Handwriting can be painful and children often get into bad habits by forming letters incorrectly. You will need to monitor the way that children form their letters and not just the final presentation. We recommend that handwriting is taught in small groups so that the teacher can observe the children's letter formation very carefully. You will also need to make sure that your own letter formation follows the format of the handwriting scheme that is being used in the school. You will need to pay very careful attention to the way in which you model letter formation, and in particular you will need to ensure that you start the letter in the correct place.

Critical questions

» *Given the growth of technology such as word-processing software, computers, laptops and tablets for writing, how important is it to teach handwriting in the twenty-first century?*

» *Some schools teach pupils a cursive style of handwriting right from the start of their formal education. What are the arguments for and against this?*

» *Should teachers ask pupils to redraft their work if the handwriting is untidy, even when the content of the writing is excellent?*

The national curriculum (2013) introduces pupils to the diagonal and horizontal joining strokes in Year 2. In the non-statutory guidance there is a recommendation that pupils should be taught to write with a joined style as soon as they can form letters correctly with the correct orientation.

Critical points

» *Children should be encouraged to apply their knowledge of phonics to help them to spell words.*

» *Spelling should be taught through rich multi-sensory teaching.*

» *Pupils may be able to read more words than they can spell.*

» *One method of teaching spelling may not work for all pupils. Select approaches which have the greatest impact on individual pupils.*

» *Correct modelling of letter formation is vital.*

» *With young children handwriting is best taught is smaller groups so that you can monitor letter formation.*

» *Handwriting needs to be taught through multi-sensory approaches.*

Chapter reflections

This chapter has emphasised the importance of teaching spelling and handwriting through a multi-sensory approach. It has also emphasised that one size might not fit all children – one approach to teaching spelling might not work for all pupils and you will need to use a range of approaches to support children's development. Finally, we wish to emphasise the importance of adopting a supportive approach to the teaching of both spelling and handwriting to ensure that children become confident. You should praise them for their attempts and place emphasis on the quality of their ideas rather than overly focusing on the spelling and presentation. Children who find spelling particularly difficult should be supported through individual and small group intervention. However, lack of ability in spelling or handwriting should never become a barrier to learning. In these instances you can exploit the use of technological tools such as electronic spell-checkers, computers, tablets and laptops to support pupils' writing so that they can still express their ideas coherently.

Taking it further

Medwell, J, and Wray, D (2008) Handwriting: A Forgotten Language Skill. *Language and Education*, 22(1): 34–47.

O'Sullivan, O, and Thomas, A (2007) *Understanding Spelling*. London: The Centre for Literacy in Primary Education.

References

Department for Education (DfE) (2013) *The National Curriculum in England: Key Stages 1 and 2 Framework Document*. London: DfE.

Glazzard, J, and Stokoe, J (2013) *Teaching Systematic Synthetic Phonics and Early English*. Northwich: Critical Publishing.

8 Writing: transcription – Key Stage 2

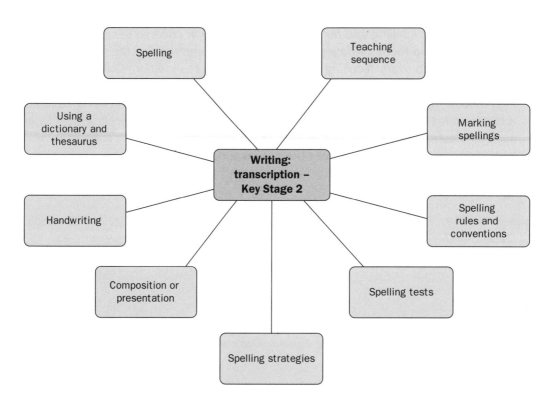

Teachers' Standards

TS3: Demonstrate good subject and curriculum knowledge

Trainees must:

*   have a secure knowledge of the relevant subject(s) and curriculum areas, foster and maintain pupils' interest in the subject, and address misunderstandings.

National curriculum links

The national curriculum states that:

> *Joined handwriting should be the norm; pupils should be able to use it fast enough to keep pace with what they want to say. Pupils' spelling of common words should be correct, including exception words and other words they have learned. Pupils should spell words as accurately as possible using their phonic knowledge and other knowledge of spelling, such as morphology and etymology.*

(DfE, 2013, p 28)

Statutory requirements for Years 3–4

Spelling

Pupils should be taught to:

- *use further prefixes and suffixes and understand how to add them (English Appendix 1 of the national curriculum);*

- *spell further homophones;*

- *spell words that are often misspelt (English Appendix 1 of the national curriculum);*

- *place the possessive apostrophe accurately in words with regular plurals (eg girls', boys') and in words with irregular plurals (eg children's);*

- *use the first two or three letters of a word to check its spelling in a dictionary;*

- *write from memory simple sentences, dictated by the teacher, that include words and punctuation taught so far.*

Handwriting

Pupils should be taught to:

- *use the diagonal and horizontal strokes that are needed to join letters and understand which letters, when adjacent to one another, are best left unjoined;*

- *increase the legibility, consistency and quality of their handwriting, eg by ensuring that the downstrokes of letters are parallel and equidistant; that lines are spaced sufficiently so that the ascenders and descenders of letters do not touch.*

(DfE, 2013, pp 31–32)

Statutory requirements for Years 5–6

Spelling

Pupils should be taught to:

- *use further prefixes and suffixes and understand the guidelines for adding them;*

- *spell some words with 'silent' letters, (eg knight, psalm, solemn);*

- *continue to distinguish between homophones and other words which are often confused;*

- *use knowledge of morphology and etymology in spelling and understand that the spelling of some words needs to be learned specifically, as listed in English Appendix 1 in the national curriculum;*

- *use dictionaries to check the spelling and meaning of words;*

- *use the first three or four letters of a word to check spelling, meaning or both of these in a dictionary;*

- *use a thesaurus.*

Handwriting and presentation

Pupils should be taught to:

- *write legibly, fluently and with increasing speed by:*

    - *choosing which shape of letter to use when given choices and deciding, as part of their personal style, whether or not to join specific letters;*

    - *choosing the writing implement that is best suited for a task.*

(DfE, 2013, pp 37–38)

Introduction

This chapter looks more closely at the term transcription and the skills that it demands both for you as a teacher and for the children as learners. The national curriculum (DfE, 2013) concentrates on spelling and handwriting and these are the focus of this chapter. However, while these are fundamental to the transcription process, it is important that you consider their impact on the bigger picture of literacy in terms of both writing and reading:

> *The term spelling refers not only to the act of writing a word, but also to the product that is written. People not only write spellings, but also read spellings, so it is not surprising that reading words and spelling words are very closely related.*

(Ehri, 2002, p 179)

Therefore understanding the mechanics of spelling improves reading (see Chapter 4). How then does spelling sit in relation to writing? Writing is a demanding process and its primary purpose is to communicate ideas to an audience. To do this, a child must choose the appropriate form and correct layout, attend to spelling, grammar, punctuation and handwriting (Medwell et al, 2014, p 122). They will also have a message that they want to share (composition Chapter 10) and they must orchestrate these two dimensions of transcription and composition to be successful. Just as with reading, these dimensions can be presented in a simple view:

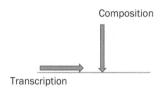

This concept has been explored and represented in a number of forms (Berninger, 2002; Brien, 2012), but this simple view with two dimensions can be most useful. Neither transcription nor composition can work in isolation if children are to succeed as written communicators. However, the skills of transcription must be taught explicitly and, just as with your teaching of phonics, you need to adopt a systematic approach.

Spelling

Critical questions

» *What are your memories of being taught to spell?*

» *Do these memories revolve around investigation and lively interactive lessons or do they focus on spelling tests?*

'Giving children spellings to learn may lull us into thinking that we are teaching spelling' (Waugh et al, 2013, p 49). It is crucial that you see spelling as learning about words, not learning words. After all, if you consider the number of words that exist in the English language it is clear that we cannot 'learn' or memorise them all. Through clearly focused and enjoyable lessons the goal is to develop an enthusiasm for language and a curiosity about words. This understanding of how words relate to one another allows children to apply their knowledge of known words to new words and so enrich the language that they use. They become ambitious rather than safe spellers.

Critical questions

» *What do you think it means to be a good speller?*

» *Is good spelling about accuracy, word choice or the understanding of rules and conventions, or is it a combination of all these elements?*

Teaching sequence

Just as with the teaching of phonics in Key Stage 1, there needs to be a structure to the teaching of spelling and the approach advocated in the DfE publication *Support for Spelling* (DCSF, 2009) allows children to construct their knowledge systematically over time:

- revisit and use;

- teach and define;

- practise and investigate;

- apply and assess.

As they revisit prior knowledge, children are able to transfer skills to new learning, and through their own investigation begin to apply new learning into their writing. Consider the following sequence of lessons in a mixed Year 3/4 class exploring the spelling patterns related to the formation of plurals.

CASE STUDY

A series of lessons

Revisit and use

Danielle revises the terms singular and plural along with the term suffix. The children are prompted to contribute what they already know about singular and plural and to collect examples and use them in sentences. They collect or are reminded of the following rules:

- Most nouns add 's' in the plural.

- Nouns ending in a hissing, buzzing or shushing sound ('ss', 'z', 'ch', 'sh') add 'es' in the plural.

- Nouns ending in a consonant and a 'y' (*baby, jelly*) change 'y' to 'i' and add 'es'.

- Nouns ending with a vowel and 'y' (*day, toy*) just add 's'.

The children then use 'show me' cards for s and es endings as words are orally explored.

Teach and define

Danielle continues by asking the children to write the plurals of given words as a quick whiteboard activity. The children are then asked to work with a partner to collect nouns ending with 'f', 'ff' or 'fe' and these words are displayed on the interactive whiteboard (eg *wolf, wife, half, cliff, thief, life*). The teacher establishes the following rules:

- Nouns ending in 'f' drop the 'f' and add 'ves' (*wolf – wolves*);

- Nouns ending in 'fe' drop the 'fe' and add 'ves' (*knife – knives*);

- Nouns ending in 'ff' just add 's' (*cliff – cliffs*).

Practise and investigate

Then the children work in groups with sets of singular words that they group according the way they change their endings when plural. The groups then design a poster to explain spelling rules for plurals. Next the children are challenged in their groups to explore other types of pluralisation:

- Irregular plurals such as *woman, child, foot*;
- Words that are the same in the singular and plural, eg *sheep*;
- Words that have no singular, eg *scissors*.

Apply and assess

Finally, Danielle reviews the rules for forming plurals and then dictates sentences using the plurals investigated:

- *The women placed the knives in the boxes on benches.*
- *The toys were washed and given to the children at the parties.*

The children are then asked to create their own sentences using given words which they then check with a partner for errors. They are asked to articulate *what they have learnt* and identify any rule that they find difficult and need to practise. These words are recorded in their spelling logs/journals and reviewed using look, cover, write, check.

Critical questions

» *In what ways do you think this structure supports learning about words?*

» *How does it develop independence?*

» *How might you use the same structure to teach placing the possessive apostrophe accurately in words with regular plurals?*

Spelling rules and conventions

Using phonic knowledge and spelling, although closely related, are different skills. The first is about making good phonetic choices, while the second is about developing an understanding of rules and conventions that can be generalised across many words. Spelling a word as it sounds is not always a reliable strategy, particularly as the child's vocabulary becomes broader. Many words have the same pronunciation, but different spellings, while many others have the same spelling but different pronunciation. Remember: in the complex alphabetic code one phoneme can be represented by different graphemes and one grapheme can represent more than one phoneme.

Don't make spelling a guessing game. It is important to share conventions with the children. It is your job to make learning as easy as possible. Consider the following.

- English words do not end in the letter 'v' unless they are abbreviations (*rev.*) Therefore if the last sound is 'v' add an 'e' – *live, above, love*.

- When an 'o' sound follows the letter 'w' it is frequently spelt with the letter 'a' – *wander, wallet, wash*.

- An 'aw' sound before an 'l' is frequently spelt with the letter 'a' – *all, ball, call, always.*

- An 'ee' sound at the end of a word is usually spelt with 'y' – *funny, lazy, mouldy.* Similarly, when choosing between 'oi' and 'oy' it is worth noting that words in English very rarely end in 'oi' and so the spelling would be 'oy', eg *enjoy.*

- When adding the prefix 'in' (meaning 'not') to a word it is important to consider the letter that the root word begins with:
  - In words beginning with 'l', 'in' becomes 'il', eg *illegal*;
  - In words beginning with 'm' or 'p', 'in' becomes 'im', eg *immortal*;
  - In words beginning with 'r', 'in' becomes 'ir', eg *irregular.*

Critical questions

» *Consider your own knowledge of the English spelling system. Were you introduced to conventions that generalise across many words or was spelling a bit of a guessing game?*

» *How could the children investigate and explore the conventions above? (Remember, we learn best when we discover, not when we are simply told.)*

» *How will you deal with exceptions to the rule?*

Activities to support the exploration of patterns and rules

It is vital that you focus on the importance of 'pattern' in words. In Key Stage 2, as the children work towards becoming accurate, independent spellers, it is this awareness of pattern that becomes all-important. Good spellers know what *usually* happens when a certain sequence of letters appear in a word. This chapter now considers some patterns that are focused on in Appendix 1 of the national curriculum at Key Stage 2 and activities to support investigation.

Card sort

When exploring common letter patterns, give the children sets of words to sort according to pronunciation (eg 'ight', 'ear', 'ough', or 'ed' when looking at words such as *jumped, wanted* or *called*).

Dictated stories

Teach a targeted spelling rule, eg the suffixes *–able* and *–ible* – the 'able' ending is far more common and is distinguished by the fact that generally if you drop the 'able' you are left with a recognisable root word, eg *enjoy – enjoyable.* Dropping 'ible' usually leaves a stem, eg *terr – terrible.* Now ask the children to record a dictated story that includes many examples of the rule. To extend, ask the children to write their own 'silly dictations'.

New words

Ask the children to invent new or nonsense words to show they can apply taught conventions, eg

- applying the double consonant rule to words where the consonant is preceded by either a short vowel (letter sound) or long vowel (letter name), ie doubling the consonant after the short vowel sound: *cratting/futted* or leaving one consonant after the long vowel sound: *hifing/woped*;

- identifying different patterns of pluralisation: *wabs/penches/covies/hubeys*.

Most common

Always give the children the opportunity to identify the most common ending when exploring suffixes such as *-tion/-able/-ear/-ight*. Although there are rules that they need to learn, it is always worth knowing the most likely option to choose when exploring new words.

Word families

Play lots of word family games, allowing the children to identify root words and derivations and see the links between words that will help them both understand and spell them, eg *cover – discover – discovery – uncover – recover – recovery*.

What comes next?

When investigating words with common letter strings, eg 'ought' and dismissing patterns that don't exist in the English language 'eaght', play this guess the word game. It is similar to hangman. You select a word containing one of the targeted letter patterns and then draw a simple picture on the board, eg a man or house. Underneath it draw dashes to indicate the number of letters in the word. Write the first letter of the word and ask for suggestions for the next letter until the word is completed. Delete part of the drawing for each incorrect suggestion.

Jokes and riddles

To support the exploration of homophones have the children explore jokes that play with the English language, eg *What is black and white and read all over? – a newspaper*.

Ask them to write riddles that reveal the meanings of words.

Marking spellings

Be careful of the attitude you convey to the children when marking spellings. The aim is not to demoralise a child, but to assess their understanding of what has been taught and to guide them to solve problems they may be facing. Not every piece of written work you mark will necessarily have a focus on accurate spelling. However, where it does, bear the following guidelines in mind.

- Set clear expectations before the children begin to write about the spelling targets they and you are aiming for. Make sure that these are matched to what the children have been taught and only mark to these shared expectations.

- Don't just focus on the errors – introduce positive marking where you reward success.

- Give the children time to read, discuss and reflect on your comments.

- Don't ask a child to write a spelling out a number of times – link it to sentence construction or handwriting. If the child is adding target words to their log/journal encourage them to use look, cover, write check.

- Set mini-targets that are achievable.

- Remind them of strategies they can use before they begin to write.

CASE STUDY

David

David is an able Year 6 child who works at above-average levels in most subjects, particularly mathematics and science. However, it is often difficult to motivate him to write beyond the bare minimum during English lessons. His teacher undertook a writing interview with David to explore his thoughts about writing and as part of the interview asked him to identify two pieces of his written work that he considered to be his best and two pieces that were less successful. The teacher found that 'best' was equated with work that had no spellings corrected and marking commenting on neatness of presentation – these were generally short pieces with specific layouts such as explanation and letters. David's less successful choices were two pieces of narrative where a number of spelling errors had been highlighted and comments such as *'concentrate on your spelling'* were recorded. David and his teacher discussed the choices, the latter saying that he thought one of the narratives was actually one of David's best pieces. David responded by saying *'Well, it doesn't say that, does it?'*

Critical questions

» *What might the teacher take away from this interview?*

» *It is important to support children in correcting their spellings, but how can you do this positively when working with reluctant writers?*

» *How can writing interviews be used to promote the development of transcription skills?*

Self-image

Accurate spelling is not an end in itself. Its purpose is to allow children to communicate effectively as writers of meaningful messages. Therefore it is important that the quest for accurate spelling doesn't become a barrier both practically and psychologically to the goal of communicating effectively and with enjoyment and confidence. Successful spellers can focus their time and energy into the skills of composition, sentence structure and precise word choice (*Support for Spelling*, p 2). Anxious spellers lose motivation, take the easy option, eg write *big* rather than *enormous* and become reluctant writers. Children who become obsessed with having the right spelling for every word have a distorted view of the 'simple view of writing'.

Critical questions

»   *Why do some children become averse to taking risks with their word choice and become safe spellers?*

»   *As teachers, how might we be responsible for this attitude and what can we do to avoid it?*

Of course, the goal is to achieve independent corrections of spellings and to do this the skill of proofreading will need to be introduced (see Chapters 9 and 10), but this independence also relies upon using the right strategies.

Spelling strategies

Chapter 7 looked at a range of strategies that children might use to support their spelling. It is important to identify the right strategies to use and to do this it is vital to acknowledge that not every speller is the same, even though the actual spellings are. The type of speller you are can generally be narrowed down into three categories: visual, auditory or learning based. This is not to say that children do not use a combination of these styles, but the majority of us do have preferred learning styles and they are worth matching to different strategies.

Visual strategies:

*   Write the given word two or three times in joined handwriting and then delete the attempts that appear visually incorrect.

*   Identify the part of the word that is 'tricky', eg s**ai**d or cha**tt**ing.

*   Look for words within words, eg ap**parent**.

*   Look, cover, write, check.

Auditory strategies:

*   Break words down into syllables and identify the phonemes in each syllable.

*   Exaggerate silent letters, eg *bus-i-ness* or *Wed-nes-day*.

*   Use analogy.

Learning-based strategies:

*   Use morphology to identify the root/prefix/suffix.

*   Use the origin of words (etymology).

- Use mnemonics.

- Learn words in groups or patterns, eg homophones – focus on groups that look the same – *where/there/here*.

- Identify the spelling rule.

Spelling tests

To test or not to test is a question that causes some controversy. There is no doubt that children's ability to generalise the rules and conventions they are taught into independent writing is crucial, but do tests dictate whether this will actually happen? The answer is categorically 'no' and many of us can score full marks in a test, then forget to use the correct spelling when we are in full compositional flow.

This is not to say that tests do not have a place, but what you should be really testing is the understanding of the rule in question rather than specific words. Here are some tips for testing.

- If you must test lists of independent words then make them 'topic words' or useful 'tricky' words (see Appendix 1 of *Support for Spelling*).

- When the children take their words home to learn make sure that it is actually the rule they are learning. Give them some examples, but when you come to test include words that were not examples but conform to the rules.

- Don't read out random words – place them into context in sentences.

- Make up silly dictations that include words from the rules and conventions being investigated. Have the children write their own silly sentences.

Using a dictionary and thesaurus

Dictionaries

Independent usage of dictionaries continues to be a focus of the national curriculum in Key Stage 2 and it is important to give children opportunities to become fluent readers of dictionaries. They need to understand how they work and when they should be used. You need to encourage the children to use their knowledge of the different options for spelling sounds and stress that they should continue their efforts to locate words when their initial search has been unsuccessful, eg the child who tries to look up *grieve* under 'gree' needs to be reminded to consider other possibilities.

Although dictionaries can support independence, they can be overused and break the flow of writing. You don't want what MacKay describes as an *'almost neurotic preoccupation with accuracy that can kill a lesson'* (MacKay, 2005). Encourage the children to underline uncertain spellings and return to checking them in a dictionary at the end of the lesson or section of writing. Again spelling checkers are useful tools if the first attempt at spelling the word was logical and reasonably close to the target; however, if this is not the case then the child may be offered inappropriate suggestions. They need to be prepared to question whether the pronunciation of the given word matches the one they are attempting to spell.

Thesaurus

There are a number of good reasons for learning how to use a thesaurus and these should be shared with the children.

* By exploring synonyms the child can avoid repetition in their writing.

* They can find the word that best expresses an idea.

* Vocabulary can be enriched and developed.

However, the use of these language tools should always be accompanied by a caution, and again the children need to be taught how to use them appropriately. They need to understand the following two points:

* Not all synonyms are equal – they do not all mean exactly the same thing.

* A *big* word is not always the *best* word.

Lots of work around 'shades of meaning' will allow the children to identify which words are appropriate and carry the meaning that will allow their reader both to visualise the picture they are painting with words and indeed to decide whether they empathise with the event or character being described. Consider these two sentences and the choice of words: *The* **chubby** *baby* **gurgled** */ The* **corpulent** *baby* **snickered**.

Critical questions

» *How do these two sentences paint different pictures of the character?*

» *Why is it important for children to explore how their choice of words impacts on their reader and what activities might you introduce for them to explore shades of meaning?*

Handwriting

Alongside spelling, the national curriculum coverage of transcription focuses on handwriting, and in Chapter 7 we focused on the importance of teaching for fluent letter formation using multi-sensory approaches.

Critical questions

» *Why does the focus on handwriting continue in Key Stage 2?*

» *Do the aims of teaching handwriting change, and if so in what ways?*

You are aiming to develop fluent and effective writers who have an impact on their readers. Just as poor spelling can become a barrier to meaningful communication, so can poor handwriting become both a real and perceived problem in terms of achieving successful outcomes. The real problem is that handwriting must be legible so that the audience can read it – illegible handwriting carries no meaning. This is also true for the authors themselves, they too need to be able to read what they have written. The perceived problem is that very often the reader makes assumptions about the quality of the message from the manner in which it is presented. They don't expect very much if the handwriting is poorly formed and the words difficult to decipher. As an author, if I make my reader work too hard they will lose interest and may ultimately give up. This lack of motivation is also reflected back to the writer, who gets little pleasure or success from the writing process. Poor transcription skills make writing a chore and the children get tired, quite literally – watch a learner who is struggling as they begin to yawn and their whole body posture droops.

CASE STUDY

Dean and Joseph

Dean, a child in Year 3, has strong oral language skills, but poor letter formation and spelling means that he struggles to record his ideas. He is working in an intervention group aimed at improving the quantity and quality of written communication. Dean is partnered with Joseph, a child who has difficulties composing coherent ideas but who has good transcriptional skills. It is thought that the two boys can support one another in their writing. After six weeks of quite intensive intervention, where the focus has been on developing oral language and ideas, there has been a marked improvement in Joseph's writing both in terms of quantity and quality. Dean, despite being prepared to write in greater length, continues to be frustrated with what he records and describes his writing as 'a mess'. It is noted that he often resorts to the repetition of sentences to meet the growing expectations for him to write at greater length.

Critical questions

»   *Why do you think Joseph has made more progress than Dean?*

»   *Does the development of oral language have an equal impact on composition and transcription?*

»   *How might Dean be supported to improve his transcription?*

The case study above suggests that it is vital to identify which dimension of the writing process needs to be addressed to improve written communication. While Joseph could 'magpie' ideas for composition, Dean could not 'magpie' Joseph's superior transcription skills without specific attention being paid to his letter formation and processing of spelling.

The more fluent the handwriting, the easier it becomes to allow ideas to flow onto a page. Your role as a teacher is to give the children the opportunity and the support to improve their handwriting skills, whatever year group they may be in. It is not just a job for the Key Stage 1 teacher. But you need to make it purposeful and not appear as a punishment: children often see handwriting practice as a monotonous exercise. Make sure that you link it to spelling focuses or the writing of final drafts for publication.

Critical questions

» *If we write for different purposes should we have different styles/expectations for different tasks?*

» *Are there times when the neatness of presentation is less important?*

Composition or presentation?

Chapter 2 explored the two functions of oral language – exploratory and presentational. It is important to consider these functions in relation to handwriting. When you give children a written task is your focus on composition or presentation? Who is the writing for? Many activities in the classroom relate to exploration and composition. When a child is generating a narrative they may change their minds several times, just as we do as adults. Sitting here at my desk writing this paragraph I notice words crossed out and arrows rearranging sentences. While my handwriting is legible it is not for presentation. At this moment in time, I am the audience and I am exploring my thoughts. Notes, first drafts and informal wonderings are very different from final drafts and formal letters.

Critical questions

» *Do you think recognising the different functions of handwriting leads to a positive attitude towards transcription?*

» *How would you make sure that the children, particularly those with poor handwriting skills, get enough practice at developing a good presentational style?*

Critical points

» *Transcription is one dimension of the writing process and works in tandem with composition.*

» *Good spellers are not safe spellers – they use their knowledge about words.*

» *Spelling needs to be taught explicitly through a systematic approach.*

» *Children need to learn about the rules and conventions of spelling in the English language.*

» *Rules and conventions should be taught through investigations that are fun and interactive.*

» *Children must be taught spelling strategies and reminded of these before they write.*

» *Handwriting needs to be fluent and legible, but you need to be aware of the different purposes for writing.*

Chapter reflections

This chapter has focused on the development of the transcriptional skills of spelling and handwriting. It has emphasised the importance of teaching these skills within the bigger picture of the writing process. There is no doubt that to be successful written communicators children have to be knowledgeable spellers and have a fluent script. It is your responsibility to tread the thin line between automatic mechanics and lively investigation. Don't allow your children to become frightened of taking risks with their spelling – you want them to be ambitious, not safe.

Taking it further

Crystal, D (2012) *Spell it Out: The Singular Story of English Spelling*. London: Profile Books.

References

Berninger, V, Vaughan, K, Abbott, Brooks, A, Begay, K, Curtin, G, et al (2002) Teaching Spelling and Composition Alone and Together: Implications for the Simple View of Writing. *Journal of Educational Psychology*, 94: 291–304.

Brien, J (2012) *Teaching Primary English*. London: Sage.

DCSF (2009) *Support for Spelling*. London: DCSF.

Department for Education (DfE) (2013) *The National Curriculum in England: Key Stages 1 and 2 Framework Document*. London: DfE.

Ehri, L (2002) Reading Processes, Acquisition and Instructional Implications, in Reid, G and Wearmouth, J (eds) *Dyslexia and Literacy: Theory & Practice*, Chichester: John Wiley & Sons.

MacKay, N (2005) *Removing Dyslexia as a Barrier to Achievement: The Dyslexia Friendly School Toolkit*. Wakefield: SEN Marketing.

Medwell, J A, Wray, D, Moore, G E, and Griffiths, V (2014) *Primary English: Theory & Practice* (7th edn). London: Learning Matters Ltd.

Waugh, D Warner, C, and Waugh, R (2013) *Teaching Grammar, Punctuation and Spelling in Primary School*. London: Learning Matters.

9 Writing: composition – Key Stage 1

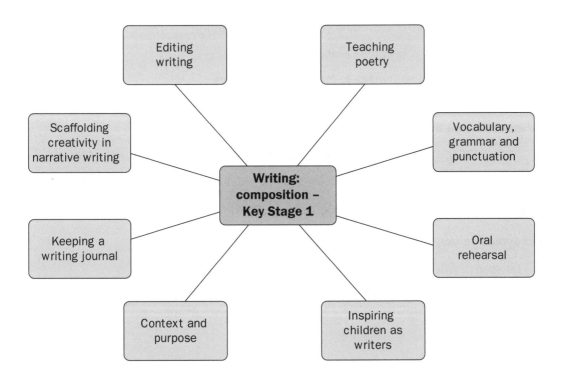

Teachers' Standards

TS3: Demonstrate good subject and curriculum knowledge

Trainees must:

- have a secure knowledge of the relevant subject(s) and curriculum areas, foster and maintain pupils' interest in the subject, and address misunderstandings.

National curriculum links

Writing

The national curriculum states that:

> Effective composition involves forming, articulating and communicating ideas, and then organising them coherently for a reader. This requires clarity, awareness of the audience, purpose and context, and an increasingly wide knowledge of vocabulary and grammar.
>
> (DfE, 2013, p 15)

Statutory requirements for pupils in Year 1

Pupils should be taught to:

- Write sentences by:
    - saying out loud what they are going to write about;
    - composing a sentence orally before writing it;
    - sequencing sentences to form short narratives;
    - rereading what they have written to check that it makes sense;
- discuss what they have written with the teacher or other pupils;
- read aloud their writing clearly enough to be heard by their peers and the teacher.

(DfE, 2013, p 24)

Statutory requirements for pupils in Year 2

Pupils should be taught to:

- Develop positive attitudes towards and stamina for writing by:
    - writing narratives about personal experiences and those of others (real and fictional);
    - writing about real events;
    - writing poetry;
    - writing for different purposes;
- Consider what they are going to write before beginning by:
    - planning or saying out loud what they are going to write about;
    - writing down ideas and/or key words, including new vocabulary;
    - encapsulating what they want to say, sentence by sentence;

- *Make simple additions, revisions and corrections to their own writing by:*

  - *evaluating their writing with the teacher and other pupils;*

  - *rereading to check that their writing makes sense and that verbs to indicate time are used correctly and consistently, including verbs in the continuous form;*

  - *proofreading to check for errors in spelling, grammar and punctuation (eg ends of sentences punctuated correctly);*

- *reading aloud what they have written with appropriate intonation to make the meaning clear.*

(DfE, 2013, p 31)

Introduction

Many pupils find the task of writing challenging because they have not yet reached the stage of automaticity. Children often have brilliant ideas which they are able to articulate very effectively. However, beginning writers cannot simply focus on recording their ideas on paper and developing them further into powerful texts which engage the reader. This is because they also have to consciously think about aspects such as spelling, handwriting and punctuation at the same time as developing *ideas* and this can slow down the process of composition. As pupils develop automaticity in applying the skills of spelling, handwriting and punctuation they can then focus their attention on developing ideas which draw the reader into the text and they can start to consider the use of vocabulary, grammar and punctuation to create powerful effects.

We want children to see themselves as writers and authors of their own work. In order to develop children's confidence in writing it is important that their attempts at writing are valued. As a trainee teacher you need to ensure that you give children credit for their *ideas* even when their spelling, handwriting and punctuation require attention. Although it is important that these aspects are addressed systematically over time through high-quality teaching and clear target setting, great authors are all able to use writing as a tool to make a connection with the reader. Caulley (2008) emphasises the importance of writing stories which give the reader a *'sense that the action is unfolding in front of them – that the reader is part of the scene. The reader hears the conversation, sees the gestures, and follows the actions of the characters'* (p 429). Ideas and the use of vocabulary, grammar and punctuation *for effect* are important in writing because they help the writer to make this significant connection with the reader. If children are to view themselves as authors they need to be able to recognise that great ideas and writing for effect are essential ingredients of powerful texts.

This chapter will introduce you to some fundamental principles of teaching early composition. It will not address everything you need to know about teaching writing, but it will provide you with a basis for your approach to teaching writing.

Oral rehearsal

In the early stages of becoming writers children need to be supported to rehearse their ideas orally before they write. Some pupils do not speak in sentences and if children are unable to *say* a sentence then they will almost certainly find it impossible to *write* a sentence. In EYFS and Year 1 you need to model this process to children because they are unlikely to use oral rehearsal automatically. When you model the process of writing a sentence to young children the following steps will help you to address this very systematically.

- **Think it:** explicitly model thinking of a sentence.
- **Say it:** say the sentence out loud.
- **Count the words:** count the number of words in the sentence.
- **Write it:** write the sentence word by word.
- **Read it aloud:** does it make sense? Can I improve it?
- **Check it:** have I got the correct number of words? Have I got a capital letter at the start of my sentence? Have I got a space between each word? Have I got a full stop at the end of my sentence?

If children observe you following this process then they will gradually start to use it in their own writing. There is a clear expectation in the national curriculum (DfE, 2013) that pupils in Year 1 should be writing in sentences and this process will help them to achieve this. Many pupils start to write something without fully thinking through the sentence beforehand. You need to encourage them to lock the sentence into their head and say it out loud before they write it. This process should be repeated for every sentence that children attempt to write so that they get into the habit of using a systematic approach to their writing. Some pupils in your class may not be writing in sentences and these pupils will need extra support, particularly in Year 1, to support them to achieve this.

The process of oral rehearsal can be developed further as pupils become more confident in writing longer texts. Pupils should be given time to think through their ideas before they start to compose any form of writing. Great writing cannot be rushed and it evolves over time. Once they have thought through their ideas, pupils should then be encouraged to plan their writing using a systematic approach. More information about planning writing is included later in this chapter. Once pupils have had time to think and plan, they should be given an opportunity to rehearse their ideas orally with a response partner. Working with their response partner, they can then build on their initial ideas to improve them and annotate their plans accordingly to demonstrate the changes that have been made. Collecting feedback from their peers in this way is important because the best writing is often produced through a process of collaboration rather than in isolation. Peers can be a valuable source of advice to a writer. They can suggest ideas to make the writing more interesting and exciting and they can give the author an insight into how the reader might respond to the writing before the text has actually been written. They can suggest better words to use and ways of improving the presentation and layout. In the case of writing narratives, a response partner can provide feedback on the characters, the build-up, climax, resolution or ending and this can help to improve the story. You need to teach your pupils that the best authors are like magpies who steal ideas from other people to make their writing better.

The process described above takes time. If you want pupils to produce good-quality writing then you cannot expect this to happen within the space of a one-hour lesson. You need to think of teaching composition more in terms of a sequence of lessons; each lesson builds progressively on the previous one so that at the end of that unit of work pupils have a quality piece of writing they can be proud of. Generating good ideas is not a process which should be rushed and children need to be taught that their best ideas might take time to develop.

Modelling oral rehearsal

You also need to *teach* children how to give supportive and constructive feedback to each other on their writing. You will need to think carefully about how you intend to pair children up: will you use same-ability, mixed-ability or friendship pairs and will the pairs be fixed or flexible? You need to model the process of orally rehearsing your own writing and receiving feedback on it. One way of doing this is to involve a teaching assistant (TA) using the following process:

Trainee/Teacher: Discuss your ideas for your writing by talking through the plan. Ask the TA if they can help you to make it better.

TA: Talk about *several* aspects of the writing that are effective using *www* (what works well) and discuss what the author can do to make the writing even better using *ebi* (even better if ...).

Trainee/Teacher: Thank the TA for the feedback and consider whether the suggested changes will enhance the writing. If the suggestions will improve the writing then amend the plan with the new ideas by annotating it accordingly.

As children become more confident with composition they will gradually be able to receive more feedback from their response partner about their writing. However, in the early stages of composition it seems sensible to suggest that feedback is limited to one suggestion for improvement only so that children's confidence is maintained.

Critical questions

» *In the national curriculum there is a focus in Year 1 on teaching children to write in sentences using correct vocabulary, grammar and punctuation. In Year 2 teachers need to support pupils to develop stamina for writing. At this stage children are expected to write narratives, poetry and to write for different purposes. As a Year 1 teacher, how would you support and prepare your pupils for learning in Year 2?*

» *Should pupils in Year 1 be asked to write for a range of purposes?*

Inspiring children as writers: being a role model

If you are going to inspire your pupils to be writers and authors you will need to model being an author yourself. Take the time to compose your own short stories, poems and non-fiction texts. Share these with your pupils and display your own work in the classroom. Children need to recognise that writing is something we can all gain immense pleasure from. Involve your pupils in helping you to edit and improve your own work. Compose your own texts in line with the text types you are teaching at the time so that pupils have the knowledge to help you to redraft your work. Model reading your own work aloud to children and ask them for their responses to it.

Context and purpose

Setting up a context for writing is perhaps one of the most important things that you need to do. Without a context for writing, children have no clear purpose and the writing task is disconnected from other learning that is taking place in the classroom. The Ofsted report *Moving English Forward: Action to Raise Standards in English* (Ofsted, 2012) highlighted some of the weaknesses in the teaching of writing. These include:

- *too few opportunities for pupils to complete extended writing;*

- *too little time in lessons to complete writing tasks;*

- *too little emphasis on creative and imaginative tasks;*

- *too little emphasis on the teaching of editing and redrafting;*

- *too little choice for pupils in the topics for writing;*

- *too few real audiences and purposes for writing;*

(Ofsted, 2012, pp 25–26)

Additionally, the report states that:

> *Teachers need to ensure that English in classrooms integrates tasks and purposes related to the 'real world' beyond school, and includes real audiences, contexts and purposes.*

(Ofsted, 2012, para 142, p 53)

The contexts for writing in Year 1 or Year 2 could emerge from a class topic or theme, texts that children are reading or real situations in the school or in the community. Creating contexts for writing will also provide you with opportunities to make writing purposeful and link the teaching of writing to other aspects of the curriculum. Your ability to create a context for writing will largely depend on your own creative thinking. However, if you do it well you will be able to hook children into learning. A good hook will ignite children's enthusiasm for writing and they will soon be immersed and even obsessed about what they are writing. Getting children obsessed about writing is what you should be aiming to achieve in your lessons. You need to get them to want to write in the first place and then they need to sustain their engagement until they have achieved a good-quality outcome.

Getting children obsessed about learning is a characteristic of outstanding teaching. This is evident when children are not simply attentive in lessons but when they are truly engrossed in the task they are doing. Attentive pupils can equal passive learners. As a trainee teacher you need to think carefully about how you will immerse your learners in a writing task to the point where they do not want to stop writing. Creating contexts and giving children clear purposes for writing is certainly a step in the right direction and therefore a significant amount of thought needs to go into the planning of lessons. Great teachers spend as much time (if not more) thinking through their lessons as they do in writing detailed lesson plans. Time spent thinking is time well spent if it results in lessons which are set in context and ignite children's interests.

There is no correct model of how a writing lesson should be structured. There is no right way of teaching and no correct way of structuring a lesson. You should not aim to be a carbon-copy of your mentor. Develop your own style of teaching and your own educational values and beliefs. Focus on inspiring your learners by hooking them into writing. Make the writing task relevant to them and set it in context. Talk less in lessons and give them more time on task to develop their ideas. Encourage them to collaborate and persevere even when they find writing difficult. Focus on supporting them to take pride in their work and allow them opportunities to revisit it to make it better. Give them tools for learning to help them to work independently. These could include:

* working walls which display good models of text types and vocabulary;

* alphabet mats;

* dictionaries;

* a shoulder partner;

* a writing journal.

Give your learners different audiences for writing. The audience for a piece of writing is often the teacher but you need to encourage them to write to different people. Examples could include:

* writing stories, poems or non-fiction texts for the school library for others to read;

* writing a letter to the head teacher about an issue in the school;

* writing a letter to the local council about a community issue;

* creating persuasive posters to encourage parents to attend a school event;

* writing poems and displaying them around the school grounds for others to read;

* writing something for the school blog.

CASE STUDY

Setting a context for writing in Year 1

A class of Year 1 pupils are learning about space as part of a science topic. One day when they are in the hall they notice an alien standing outside. She has a green face and appears to be lost. The children are immediately hooked. The teacher asks the class if she can invite the alien in to talk to them. She asks the children to work in pairs to write down questions that they want to ask the alien. The teacher then brings the alien into the hall and a hot-seating session follows. The children want to know:

- *Where have you come from?*
- *What is your name?*
- *What is it like on your planet?*
- *What do you eat?*
- *What are your hobbies?*
- *Are you a nice alien?*

The alien then disappears and the children return to their classroom. In the classroom they find the head teacher and they inform her that they have just met an alien. She does not believe them. The head teacher says *'If you have really seen an alien you are going to have to write me a description of it otherwise I will just think you have been dreaming!'* The pupils agree to write character descriptions and these are then shared with the head teacher.

CASE STUDY

Setting a context for writing in Year 2

This example draws on an approach known as *Mantle of the Expert* invented by Dorothy Heathcote in the 1980s. The approach uses drama to place children into the position of being experts. They are encouraged to make decisions and take control of their learning.

Year 2 pupils have been reading the story of *Little Red Riding Hood*. The teacher enters the classroom in role as the mother. She has received a telephone call to inform her that the woods are being taken over by wolves, and as it is the only way to grandma's house she is worried that grandma will become lonely. The town councillors want to sort this problem out as quickly as possible and in a humane way but they need good volunteers to help them. Stepping out of role, the teacher asks the class if they would be willing to help the councillors and at this point the children are hooked into the context. They agree to volunteer their help. They then design badges to denote their new roles and they write character descriptions so that people in the community know who they are. They work together in groups to discuss how they might help and what action might be taken to solve the problem with the wolves. Next they write a letter to the chief councillor to offer some solutions to the problem.

Critical questions

» *How could you develop the work for Year 2 further?*

» *To what extent do typical lesson structures in primary schools impede children's immersion in writing?*

» *Oral rehearsal, peer feedback and access to tools for learning provide pupils with support to enable them to produce quality writing. However, assessments of children's writing are carried out when pupils are working independently, often in test conditions with no access to support. What impact might this have on children's achievement in writing?*

Keeping a writing journal

Writing journals are a useful point of reference for children to support them in the writing process. The approach works well, especially in Year 2 and beyond, where pupils need to start experimenting with using a wider range of vocabulary. As children begin to read more widely they will encounter new and interesting vocabulary which they could use to improve their own writing. The writing journal could serve several purposes, including:

*   recording powerful vocabulary which pupils can then use in their own writing;

*   recording examples of story settings and associated descriptions;

*   recording example story endings;

*   recording examples of effective character descriptions;

*   recording synonyms, for example alternative words for *said*.

Children need to borrow ideas from other people's work to improve their writing. They need to know that this is exactly what good writers do.

Scaffolding creativity in narrative writing

Some pupils find it difficult to compose a story from scratch. This is because teachers sometimes ask them to compose stories before they have had the opportunity to build up their knowledge of well-known stories. Good authors read widely, and through reading a range of texts, they build up a large repertoire of ideas for their own writing. Initially in EYFS and Year 1 children need to be introduced to well-known stories. They need to be given various opportunities to retell these stories and they need to consolidate their understanding of these stories through role play, drama and other creative opportunities. At this age, pupils need opportunities to listen to digital versions of stories and to explore re-enacting stories using puppets. Once pupils have become familiar with well-known stories they will start to retell these stories orally and they will begin to internalise the story language used in these texts. This vocabulary should then start to appear in their writing.

Once familiarity has been established with well-known stories you can teach children to adapt these by making some small changes to the original text. This could include:

*   changing the setting where the story takes place;

*   substituting one character for another;

*   changing an event;

*   changing the ending;

*   adding in new events;

*   changing the title.

You can teach children to work within the framework of the original text, but by making a change, the story becomes their story. However, the original story acts as a scaffold so that pupils are not expected to create a story from nothing.

As pupils develop their confidence in adapting stories by creating new settings, characters, events or endings they will gradually develop the ability to invent their own stories. However, even at this stage, children are not creating a story from nothing. They will have read and listened to a wide range of stories. They will have developed a bank of ideas and vocabulary in their writing journals and they will be able to rehearse their ideas orally with their peers.

Editing writing

Great authors never produce a perfect piece of writing the first time. They reread their work, edit it and make it better, and this is a process we need to teach pupils. The national curriculum (DfE, 2013) states that pupils in Year 2 must be taught to evaluate their writing to check that it makes sense and to proofread it for errors in spelling, grammar and punctuation.

You must model this process of editing to pupils, particularly during shared writing with the whole class. After the pupils have helped you to compose a class text you can ask them to reread it to check firstly for sense and secondly for accuracy in spelling, grammar and punctuation. You can then involve the pupils in making decisions about how to make the writing even better, for example by adding additional descriptive vocabulary.

CASE STUDY

Joseph's editing

A Year 2 class have been to a zoo and have been asked to write a recount of the experience. Joseph has produced a correctly punctuated account with accurate spelling but the account switches from past to present tense. In the feedback, the teacher identifies what Joseph has done well. Joseph is then given a target which asks him to ensure that he has used past tense consistently throughout the account. The teacher provides Joseph with an example of two sentences in the feedback; one is written in the present tense and one is written in the past tense. The next day Joseph is given time to read the feedback and an opportunity to make changes to his writing. Using a 'polishing pen' (a green pen) Joseph then changes the present-tense verbs into past tense to improve his account.

Critical questions

» *In the above case study, Joseph is a passive recipient of feedback. How can you encourage pupils to take a more active role in evaluating and editing their own work?*

» *Should teachers display pupils' initial drafts of writing or just final edited pieces of work? What are the arguments for and against displaying initial drafts?*

When pupils are writing and editing their work they need to be encouraged to *write as a reader*. They need to consciously think about their writing and the impact that it will have on the reader. They also need to think how they can create a better impact on the reader through making better vocabulary choices, adding description or including punctuation for effect.

Teaching poetry

There is an emphasis in the national curriculum on teaching children to recite poetry by heart from Year 1, but children are not expected to write poetry until Year 2. The processes described above for narrative texts should also support you in teaching poetry. Pupils need opportunities to listen to and read a range of different types of poetry. They need to be given opportunities to learn poems by heart and to perform them. Once children are familiar with poetry, they should be given opportunities to adapt existing poems and rhymes by altering some of the words. This will enable them to create their own version of a poem within a framework which already exists. Once pupils have had opportunities to adapt poems, they should be taught how to create their own poems.

Different types of poems have their own structural and language features and you need to model these to pupils through processes such as shared writing. Children should not be asked to write an acrostic poem unless they have had opportunities to read acrostic poetry and the opportunity to contribute to creating a class acrostic poem. Modelling clearly plays a very important role in all teaching because children cannot be expected to produce high-quality work unless they have seen good examples and been given opportunities to create these as a class or in smaller groups.

Children's knowledge of noun phrases (for example, *the blue butterfly*) for description and specification, tense, adjectives and adverbs can all be used to create effects in poetry. Children need to explore the world through all of their senses using first-hand experiences; a poem about a season, for example, will be far richer if children have been given opportunities to observe, touch, hear, taste and smell things that specifically relate to that season. Exploring the world through senses is a powerful way of generating descriptive vocabulary. Once this vocabulary has been generated, children can then use it to write simple poems.

In addition to exploring the real world through senses, children can explore the imagined world through role play, drama and technology. Immersive space technology enables children to explore settings which they would otherwise not be able to. Through pop-up mini immersive spaces or large immersive spaces which fill a school hall or classroom, children can be taken into places such as space, deserts, rain forests and beaches. A drama lesson within an immersive space can provide a stimulus for a poetry lesson or a lesson on writing a story setting. If we expose children to rich experiences such as these prior to writing, the quality of their work will be far superior because they will have experienced the sights, sounds and even smells of that setting before we ask them to write about them in a poem.

Vocabulary, grammar and punctuation

The national curriculum (DfE, 2013) identifies very specific statutory content which must be taught in each year group in relation to grammar (word, sentence and text level) and punctuation. In Year 1, pupils need to be introduced to the effects of adding prefixes and suffixes onto words and they need to understand the meaning of specific terminology including *verb*, *clause* and *pronoun*. In Year 2, pupils need to understand terminology including *noun*, *noun phrase*, *adverb*, *tenses*, and teachers need to teach pupils about conjunctions. These terms are explained in the glossary.

The aim of developing children's knowledge of grammar and punctuation for effect is for them to produce more sophisticated writing which makes an impact on the reader. Although pupils will need specific lessons on adverbs, verbs, nouns, noun phrases, adjectives and so on, you will also need to draw attention to the ways in which writers use grammar and punctuation in their texts during shared and guided reading sessions. When grammar and punctuation are taught within context, pupils are then able to see how writers have used it to create a more profound effect on the reader. This is known as *reading as a writer*. This process focuses on encouraging children to think carefully about the impact the writer is trying to have on the reader through the choice of specific vocabulary and punctuation.

Critical questions

» *What are the arguments for and against teaching grammar through decontextualised grammar exercises?*

» *What are the arguments for and against teaching punctuation through decontextualised punctuation exercises?*

» *Should punctuation and grammar only be taught in the context of texts?*

Games for Key Stage 1 Grammar – making it concrete

Basketful of nouns

The children literally take a basket or container and collect objects, naming them as they do. This can be adapted to support phonic knowledge as they collect objects/nouns beginning with specific sounds.

Scream and shout

The children physically explore acting out the verbs so that they can identify them as *doing words*. Depending on the focus, change the name of the game – this title could focus on exploring 'speech verbs', but Creep and Crawl would focus on verbs for movement.

Adjective tennis

Working in pairs, the children focus on different themed adjectives, eg colour or size. They take it in turns to 'serve' an adjective to each other, eg *big – small, tiny – huge*. Make it tricky:

introduce alphabetical tennis where each adjective must begin with the next letter of the alphabet, eg *amazing, beautiful, creepy, daft.*

Find your partner

Have two sets of cards: on one set have the names of word classes – noun, adjective and verb. On the second set have examples of these word classes – *table, run, yellow.* The children walk around the space and match their cards. Point out that nouns and verbs can be confused, eg *fish, run* and *laugh* can be either depending on their function in a sentence. Add 'to' in front of the verb to support at first, but then take it away and ask the children to justify their choice by putting their word into context within a sentence.

Critical points

» Teachers need to be authors and writers if they expect their pupils to assume this role.

» Children need stimulating contexts for writing which engage them.

» Children need clear purposes for writing.

» Children need to write for different audiences.

» Teachers should encourage children to think of a sentence and say the sentence before writing it.

» Oral rehearsal is a critical process in composition.

» Teachers need to give children sufficient time to produce their best quality writing.

» Grammar and punctuation need to be taught within the context of texts as well as discretely.

» Good writers are magpies who steal other people's ideas to make their writing better.

Chapter reflections

This chapter has emphasised the importance of praising children's ideas, even when spelling, grammar, sentence structure and punctuation require attention. The success of great writers is based on the ideas that they have composed in their texts. The capacity of texts to connect with and engage the reader is critical because work which fails to make a connection, work which does not engage and work which fails to absorb the reader into the scene is unlikely to be published. Computers can address many errors in spelling, grammar and punctuation but they cannot generate the great ideas which come out of the minds of creative writers. That said, children do clearly need to be able to spell, punctuate and write using correct grammar. Once these skills are firmly embedded, this frees children up to be able to concentrate on using writing as a vehicle for expressing ideas. Ensuring that the basic skills are embedded helps children to achieve automaticity in their writing.

Taking it further

Brien, J (2012) *Teaching Primary English*. London: Sage.

Roberts, H (2012) *Oops! Helping Children Learn Accidentally*. Carmarthen: Independent Thinking Press.

References

Caulley, D N (2008) Making Qualitative Research Reports Less Boring: The Techniques of Writing Creative Non-Fiction. *Qualitative Inquiry*, 14(3): 424–49.

Department for Education (DfE) (2013) *The National Curriculum in England: Key Stages 1 and 2 Framework Document*. London: DfE.

Office for Standards in Education (2012) *Moving English Forward: Action to Raise Standards in English*. Manchester: Ofsted.

10 Writing: composition – Key Stage 2

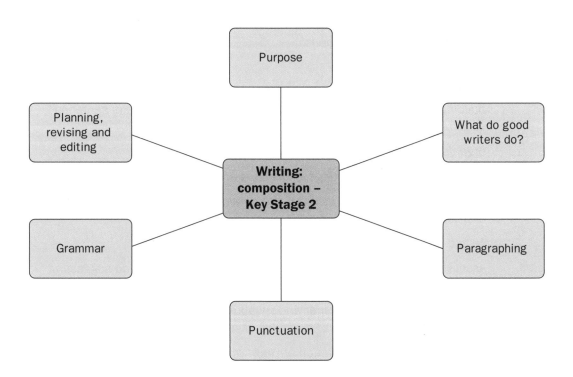

Teachers' Standards

TS3: Demonstrate good subject and curriculum knowledge

Trainees must:

- have a secure knowledge of the relevant subject(s) and curriculum areas, foster and maintain pupils' interest in the subject, and address misunderstandings.

National curriculum links

The national curriculum states that:

> *In Key Stage 2 teachers should be consolidating pupils' writing skills, their vocabulary, their grasp of sentence structure and their knowledge of linguistic terminology. Teaching them to develop as writers involves teaching them to enhance the effectiveness of what they write as well as increasing competence.*
>
> (DfE, 2013, p 28)

Statutory requirements for pupils in Years 3–4

Pupils should be taught to:

- *Plan their writing by:*

    - *discussing writing similar to what they are planning to write in order to understand and learn from its structure, vocabulary and grammar;*

    - *discussing and recording ideas;*

- *Draft and write by:*

    - *composing and rehearsing sentences orally (including dialogue), progressively building a varied and rich vocabulary and an increasing range of sentence structures (English Appendix 2 in the national curriculum);*

    - *organising paragraphs around a theme;*

    - *in narratives, creating settings, characters and plot;*

    - *in non-narrative material, using simple organisational devices (eg headings and sub-headings);*

- *Evaluate and edit by:*

    - *assessing the effectiveness of their own and others' writing and suggesting improvements;*

    - *proposing changes to grammar and vocabulary to improve consistency, including the accurate use of pronouns in sentences;*

- *Proofread for spelling and punctuation errors;*

- *Read aloud their own writing, to a group or the whole class, using appropriate intonation and controlling the tone and volume so that the meaning is clear.*

(DfE, 2013, p 25)

Statutory requirements for pupils in Years 5–6

Pupils should also be taught to:

- *Plan their writing by:*

- *identifying the audience for and purpose of the writing, selecting the appropriate form and using other similar writing as models for their own;*

- *noting and developing initial ideas, drawing on reading and research where necessary;*

- *in writing narratives, considering how authors have developed characters and settings in what they have read, listened to or seen performed;*

- *Draft and write by:*

  - *selecting appropriate grammar and vocabulary, understanding how such choices can change and enhance meaning;*

  - *in narratives, describing settings, characters and atmosphere and integrating dialogue to convey character and advance the action;*

  - *précising longer passages;*

  - *using a wider range of devices to build cohesion within and across paragraphs;*

  - *using further organisational and presentational devices to structure texts and to guide the reader (eg headings, bullet points, underlining);*

- *Evaluate and edit by:*

  - *assessing the effectiveness of their own and others' writing;*

  - *proposing changes to vocabulary, grammar and punctuation to enhance effects and clarify meaning;*

  - *ensuring the consistent and correct use of tense throughout a piece of writing;*

  - *ensuring the correct subject and verb agreement when using singular and plural, distinguishing between the language of speech and writing and choosing the appropriate register.*

(DfE, 2013, p 33)

Introduction

Chapter 8 introduced you to the simple view of writing and the two dimensions of transcription and composition that children must master to become successful, independent writers. This chapter continues to explore composition and the goal of preparing pupils to meet the demands of secondary education (DfE, 2013, p 34). It explores what good writers do as they develop their knowledge of grammar, punctuation and text cohesion and how planning, revising and editing writing that has purpose enables them to become effective communicators who influence their audience. It is your responsibility as a teacher to ensure that all of this is achieved through enjoyable and stimulating lessons that lead to your pupils seeing themselves as writers; it is your job to give them a voice.

What do good writers do?

- They enjoy writing and find the process creative, enriching and fulfilling.

- They read widely and recognise good writing.

- They understand the features of different genres of writing and are able to apply them to their own writing.

- They have something to say and write with purpose for an identified audience.

- They know how to plan.

- They make good choices about sentence structure and vocabulary that give their writing impact.

- They can reflect, revise and edit their own writing to improve this impact.

- They read as writers and write as readers – they have a voice.

All of these characteristics and skills have to be taught and modelled by you if the children are to apply them in their own writing.

Grammar

Critical question

» *Can you remember being taught grammar at primary school? If so, was it taught explicitly? How were you encouraged to apply your grammatical knowledge to your independent writing?*

Grammar has an increasingly high profile in the primary curriculum, with statutory testing for pupils at the end of Key Stage 2 (SPaG). What is meant by the term grammar? Understanding grammar is being able to talk about what it is you do when you construct sentences – to describe what the rules are and what happens when they fail to apply (Crystal, 2009). The crucial word here is 'construct', and later this chapter focuses on this idea of construction and how it relates to the demands of writing.

First, however, it is important to agree that without grammar our language does not make sense. When small children begin to communicate they develop the understanding that individual words carry meaning and that these words need to be organised together into sentences to communicate our thoughts and needs to others. As this need to communicate develops they recognise how sentences can be 'glued' together to form coherent narratives and dialogues. This spoken language is then slowly applied to their ability to record in writing, and new rules and conventions are discovered that differentiate between the spoken and written word. When we write, the audience for our thoughts is rarely standing in front of us and so non-verbal communication cannot aid the dialogue – the written words must carry all the meaning. When we begin to explore written grammar, it follows a similar course to our oral acquisition and can be broken down into three key areas: word, sentence and text.

Word

There are many word classes: nouns, verbs, adjectives, adverbs, pronouns, prepositions, determiners and conjunctions. There is not space here to look at them all in detail and you must review your own understanding of these terms. However, it is important to consider two vital points when exploring word classes with children. Firstly, the function of words is not fixed and can change according to how they are used within a sentence. Consider the word *fast* and its function in the following sentences:

The family observed the fast. (noun)
The fast car sped along the motorway. (adjective)
I fast during the religious festival. (verb)
He moved very fast across the open ground. (adverb)

The second point is that it is not enough for children to learn the definitions of these words – many children can tell you, for example, that an adverb adds more information to the verb, but do they understand that it can tell you how, where or when an action took place? Understanding is crucial if children are to apply and extend their own usage in their writing.

Sentence

Children are taught that a sentence is a group of words that go together to make sense of an individual thought or idea – a set of words that is complete in itself. However, what does this actually mean? Within a sentence there are smaller chunks of sense:

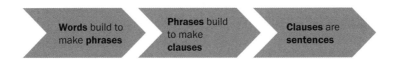

Phrases were considered in Chapter 4 and in particular the adverbial phrase, which is particularly powerful in adding detail of the how, where and when of a message. Now turn your attention to the term 'clause'. A clause contains a subject and a verb, eg *She fled.* This is a sentence in its simplest form – it is a main clause and a simple sentence consists of one main clause that can stand alone and make sense. There are three types of sentences that children must identify and use: simple, compound and complex. These will be defined in the following section, but first see if you can identify which of these three types of sentences this is:

At midnight on Friday, the young girl fled from the royal ball, rather tearfully, along the moon-lit path in front of the castle.

Although it may seem quite complicated because it has three adverbial phrases, this is in fact a **simple sentence**; it is not grammatically complex. As long as there is only one verb (*fled*), there is only one clause. It is the construction of the message and the choices available that you need to explore. The emphasis here is on construction and grammar. Children are often put off writing by the actual act of writing itself – too much, too soon. If they are learning about the correct and most effective use of grammar it should be an exercise in co-construction where you take on the role of scribe in the early stages. They are busy developing their understanding of word modification and the control of sentence structure.

Simple sentences

Oral construction

When constructing simple sentences with children you should begin by orally composing and modifying sentences through question-and-answer activities as you record the children's ideas.

Example

> Begin with the simplest of sentences:
> The cat walked.
> T: *Can you give an adjective to describe the cat?*
> C: *The fat cat walked.*
> T: *How did the fat cat walk?* (adverb)
> C: *Slowly the fat cat walked.*
> T: *Where did the fat cat slowly walk?* (adverbial phrase)
> C: *Slowly the fat cat walked up the hill.*
> T: *Can you think of a more powerful verb?* (word modification)
> C: *Slowly the fat cat meandered up the hill.*
> T: *When did the fat cat meander up the hill?* (adverbial phrase)
> C: *At midnight, the fat cat slowly meandered up the hill.*

Cut-up sentences

Follow on from the above activity by writing the original simple sentence *the cat walked* on a strip of card. Depending on your focus, collect from the children as many adjectives, adverbs, alternative verbs, adverbial phrases as they can generate and write them on to lengths of different-coloured card. In Key Stage 1 you would begin with adjectives, eg *big*, *furry*, *black*. Cut the original sentence into *the* and *cat walked* and allow the children to place the adjective cards before *cat walked* to explore their choices.

Repeat the above sentence construction with adverbial phrases and encourage the children to explore the placement of the phrases. Do they have to go at the beginning of a sentence or can they go at the end or be embedded within the sentence?

> *At midnight, the big, black cat prowled through the undergrowth.*
> *The big, black cat prowled through the undergrowth at midnight.*
> *The big, black cat prowled, at midnight, through the undergrowth.*

Remember at this point the children are not writing, they are co-constructing and exploring their options. They are experimenting with sentence structure and identifying possibilities that they can then apply in writing.

To really focus on the actual sentence structure and how phrases can be moved around within the sentence repeat the above exercise, but this time use large pieces of card that the children hold aloft and physically change places with one another.

Compound sentences

A compound sentence has two or more clauses joined by a conjunction: *and, or, but* or *so*. The clauses are of equal weight and are all main clauses, eg

> *The boy sang. The girl danced.*

Each of these is a main clause (a simple sentence) and can stand independently. However, depending on the conjunction chosen, the meaning of the sentence can change:

> *The boy sang and the girl danced.*
> *The boy sang but the girl danced.*
> *The boy sang so the girl danced.*

Again we suggest that children explore the use of conjunctions in the construction of compound sentences physically with cut-up sentences before applying this new knowledge to writing.

Complex sentences

Although many children in Key Stage 1 will be writing complex sentences, it is in Key Stage 2 that the terminology of main and subordinate clauses needs to be introduced and understood. A complex sentence consists of one main clause and one or more subordinate clauses.

- A **main clause**, when removed from a sentence, makes sense on its own.

- A **subordinate clause**, when removed from a sentence, will not make sense on its own. It needs the main clause to make sense. It begins with a subordinate conjunction, eg *after, when, since, because, although*, or a relative pronoun, eg *that, which, whose, who*. It contains both a subject and a verb, but does not form a complete sentence. Instead it adds additional information to the main clause.

Subordinate clauses can go before or after the main clause:

> **When the dog barked**, *the baby woke up.*
> *The baby woke up* **when the dog barked**.

Or it may be embedded within the main clause:

> *The dog,* **which was called Rover**, *ran through the park.*

There are different types of subordinate clauses, including relative, conditional and non-finite, and you might want to review your own subject knowledge around these terms, but the important learning for the children at this point is to be able to identify main and subordinate clauses within complex sentences. Can they identify the most important part of the sentence (the main clause), or which part can be left out but still leave the sentence making sense (the subordinate clause)? Again, this is your opportunity to model this exploration for the whole class or group.

CASE STUDY

A lesson on complex sentences

Laura had a range of main and subordinate clauses on card that could be physically moved, removed or exchanged and she demonstrated to her Year 5 class how different complex sentences could be constructed. As she did so, she constantly used the appropriate grammatical language referring to subordination, relative clauses and relative pronouns. She differentiated the complexity of the sentences and targeted different ability groups within the class to confirm or dispute her choices. She then gave the groups their own sets of clauses to construct and explore, challenging them to form as many complex sentences as possible. Finally, the children were given a 'quick write' activity where they were asked to write their own complex sentence and be prepared to share it with a writing buddy by being able to deconstruct it into main and subordinate clauses.

Critical questions

» *Although the learning objective for this lesson was to write complex sentences, why did the children spend only about five minutes of the lesson actually writing?*

» *The teaching of grammar is more about constructing sentences than writing sentences – do you agree with this statement?*

» *How will you enable children to fully explore their understanding of sentence structure before asking them to commit this knowledge to paper?*

» *What are the arguments for and against the SPaG (spelling, grammar and punctuation) test in Key Stage 2?*

Text (cohesion and coherence)

Cohesion is the 'glue' that sticks sentences together. Children learn to 'glue' words together, using correct grammar and punctuation, to form meaningful sentences. They then learn how to put sentences together to form paragraphs and paragraphs together to form whole texts. Again this needs to be taught and modelled – cutting texts up and asking the children to order them is a simple way of drawing their attention to how they are linked.

However, the text must also be coherent, which means that it must be logical, well organised and easy to read and understand by its audience. Coherence, therefore, is very much related to writing as a reader. A writer needs to pull in their audience and make them want to carry on reading – it's about creating a page turner. The focus here is on impact and effect, on making choices that enrich the writing and allow it to flow.

Varying sentence types

Although children in Key Stage 2 need to be able to write complex sentences, they also need to understand that too many complicated sentences can make their writing difficult to follow. They must learn to vary their sentences and choose the most effective for the task in hand.

A long sentence is not always the best sentence, eg in adventure stories, tension is often introduced by short, sharp sentences: *A door slammed. David froze.*

Different sentence types such as questions are used to cast doubt into the reader's mind: *What was that?* And repetition is employed to give the impression of danger approaching: *He heard steps. Steps that were coming closer. Steps that echoed through the long, dark corridor behind him.*

Punctuation

> *'Let's eat, grandma,' exclaimed Little Red Riding Hood, taking the biscuits from her basket.*
> *'No, let's eat grandma,' cried the wolf.*

It is amazing how one little black mark on a page, in this case a comma, can change the whole meaning of a sentence and possibly even save lives!

Punctuation is important and children need to understand how to use it accurately and effectively. It is all about an awareness of grammatical chunks. Children first learn to demarcate simple sentences with capital letters and full stops, but then as their sentences become more complicated and complex, they must learn how to demarcate the breaks between phrases, clauses and words, to distinguish speech and add emphasis to their thoughts and ideas.

There are many punctuation marks and again you must review your own subject knowledge of what they are and how they are used. In this chapter, we are concerned with emphasising the need to engage children in purposeful investigation that can make the study of punctuation fun. They need to realise that punctuation is an art, not a science (Medwell et al, 2014) because, as you have seen, a sentence can often be punctuated in different ways.

Hearing punctuation

Children need to 'hear' when punctuation is missing or being used incorrectly. If you consider the example of Little Red Riding Hood and the wolf above it is clear that you can have some fun with identifying the different meanings. They are best identified when you read them out loud. Indeed, it will highlight to the children the importance of reading their own compositions aloud to really check whether they have used punctuation correctly. Here are some other examples, but you will have fun finding your own.

> *Mary enjoys cooking her family and her dog.*
> *The butler stood at the door and called the guests names.*

Punctuation activities

Active punctuation

Putting actions to punctuation, particularly in the early stages of acquisition, helps children remember them and physically mark their function. A popular example of this is Kung Fu punctuation and a number of examples can be viewed on YouTube.

Punctuation relay

Split the class into teams. Each team receives a poster with a number of sentences on it. Five to six sentences is a good number. The teams also receive a bag full of punctuation marks. On the command *'begin'* the children have to select punctuation marks from the bag. Each mark then needs to be placed throughout the sentences. The team that is able to place correctly all of their punctuation marks first wins the game. The points can be awarded by sentence or for completion of all the sentences. You might also want to use full paragraphs; in this case, the winning team will have to use all of their punctuation marks throughout the paragraph to be considered the winner.

Punctuation heads

This is a complicated example, but it can be as simple as you like. Give individuals or pairs a punctuation head on a sticky note. They must use all the punctuation marks on their head either in sentences that you give them or ones of their own composition. They can use punctuation marks more than once, but should not add any that do not appear on their head. Challenge them to draw punctuation heads for their partner.

Critical questions

»   *How many punctuation marks are there in the English language? Do you know them all?*

»   *How might you draw visual representations of the functions of punctuation marks to support children's understanding?*

»   *What are the most common misconceptions children have around the use of punctuation?*

Paragraphing

Paragraphing becomes important as texts become longer and more detailed. The correct use of paragraphs show that a writer knows how to 'break text up'. It is important that children understand the reasons for starting new paragraphs and don't simply see them as a clump of sentences, thinking that after a certain number of sentences it must be time for a new paragraph.

CASE STUDY

Starting new paragraphs

Katie gave her Year 4 pupils an extract from the book they had been sharing during the class story time. It was a story they knew well and had enjoyed listening to. She asked them to work in pairs to identify the paragraph breaks in the text and identify why they thought the author had chosen to introduce new paragraphs. The children read the text, made notes and then reported back with their findings. They came up with the following reasons for starting new paragraphs:

- time had moved on;

- there had been a change of scene;

- a new character had been introduced;

- a new event had occurred;

- there had been a change of speaker.

Critical questions

» *How might the investigation of paragraph breaks in existing texts impact on the children's own writing?*

» *Why would a focus on the correct use of pronouns be important to text coherence?*

» *How would you teach any of these ideas in modelled, shared and guided writing?*

Planning, revising and editing

Drafting implies more than just 'writing it in rough first'. It allows children to get to grips with planning, revision and editing.

(Medwell et al, 2014, p 123)

Planning

When you write, whether formally or informally, you formulate some type of plan. This may be quick bullet points or may be in the form of a 'web' where you jot down ideas and thoughts that are at first quite randomly arranged. You do this so as not to forget what you want to say and then you organise these thoughts and ideas into a coherent structure.

In Key Stage 2 there is an emphasis on planning that goes beyond oral rehearsal. Here the emphasis is on planning that identifies audience and purpose and selects the appropriate form based upon models that have been read, and on developing story structures in narrative and organisational devices in non-fiction materials. It will be clear from this that you will need to teach and model different forms of planning. These will include story maps, flow diagrams, story boards, grids, webs and writing frames. Perhaps the most important task you can model is the actual *use* of a completed plan when writing. Many children waste hours of planning by not actually referring to their plans during the drafting process. The plan sits in front of them while they completely reinvent the wheel of writing.

Revising

Revision is not the same thing as editing. When you revise a piece of writing you are not correcting mistakes, but making intentional changes to support coherence and effect. You need to give your pupils permission to make these changes. These may include crossing out and resequencing and your children need to see that this is an acceptable part of the process of composition. Give them opportunities to work with a 'critical friend' who reads their work and shares a reader's view, identifying phrases or sentences that they do not fully understand or structures that need rearranging for clarity. If large chunks of writing need reorganising allow the children to literally cut up their work and resequence it rather than asking them to rewrite it. Remember, composition is about construction. Make sure that you model these processes and encourage them to be your 'critical friends' as they revise a piece of writing that you have composed.

Editing

The role of an editor is to prepare a piece of writing for publication. For the child, the task is no different. They must check for accuracy in grammar, spelling and punctuation; improve word choices and prepare their final draft. This means careful proofreading and to do this successfully the children need to read their work aloud so that they can really hear and then see any errors on the page. In many ways, they are marking their own work in the same way that you might correct and highlight inaccuracies. By learning to do this for themselves, they are developing independent skills that not only feed forward into their next piece of writing, but also allow them to more fully understand and reflect on comments that you might record in their books. Editing is not easy and again you will need to support them by modelling the task in shared and guided writing.

Critical questions

»   *How could you support less-confident writers through targeted pairing?*

»   *Some settings might cause difficulties in giving permission for real revision, being overly concerned about presentation. Would you argue the case for children being treated as 'real' authors who need to make informed changes during the drafting process?*

Purpose

Children must write for many different purposes and for a range of audiences, and Chapter 9 emphasised the importance of contextualising the writing process. Without a reason to write, a child will struggle to find their voice, and with nothing to say, they are unable to communicate. It is your task to motivate and excite children to 'want' to write and to see themselves as authors.

There are hundreds of ideas that creative teachers use to stimulate the imagination, and all of the activities and techniques introduced in the following chapter on drama aim to utilise this creative 'muscle' for all areas of the curriculum, including writing. However, here are just a few ideas that incorporate technology that you might use to develop the authors in your classroom.

Using the computer

Poetry is perhaps the most accessible form of writing for all abilities, in that it plays with language in many ways and paints a myriad of pictures. Classical narrative poems such as 'The Highwayman' by Alfred Noyes or 'The Smuggler's Song' by Kipling can be explored in many ways through drama or visualisation exercises to explore character development or prequels and sequels.

Children can also write their own version of these and other well-known poems. They can, of course, write their own poems, and one particularly intriguing technique with upper Key Stage 2 children is the blind screen. The children will need proficient keyboard skills to get the most out of this, but give it a try as they really enjoy the mystery. The children set up the computer to a word-processing program and then turn off the monitor. They then begin to compose in answer to your questions.

1. Where are you? eg a river

2. What does 'it' look like? eg flowing rapidly down the mountain (no more than five words)

3. How do you feel?

4. Write one thing you can see behind you.

   Write one more.

5. What can you hear behind you?

6. What can you smell or taste?

7. Repeat: Where are you?

8. Write one thing you can see ahead.

   Write one more.

9. What can you hear in front of you?

   What can you smell or taste?

10. Repeat: Where are you?

11. How do you feel?

12. This final word becomes the title of the poem.

They then turn the monitor back on and **discover** their poem.

Using film

Writers are 'magpies' and should be given lots of opportunity to 'steal' images from extracts from film clips that they can then feed into their own writing. Have them watch the clip with their senses in mind and ask them to record what they can see and hear and what they imagine they would smell, taste and touch. Watching crockery fall in slow motion as the Titanic sinks or joining Frodo as he enters the spider's cave offer wonderful visual stimuli.

Using Skype

The children are about to hot seat a character in the usual way and have questions that they want to ask. At the last moment, introduce the idea that the character has been unable to travel, but you have a Skype link with them. They might meet Rapunzel in her tower or Kensuke on his island. It is interesting that you rarely get the disbelief that some children express when the character is being played by either you or a TA in the classroom.

Critical questions

» *How could you use technology to support composition?*

» *How does giving children the opportunity to film their own compositions support the requirements of the national curriculum?*

Critical points

» *Without grammar, our language doesn't make sense.*

» *It needs to be taught explicitly in terms of word, sentence and text, but it needs to be understood within the context of purposeful writing.*

» *Grammar is as much about constructing text as it is about writing text.*

» *Punctuation is about the awareness of grammatical chunks.*

» *Writing must be both cohesive and coherent.*

» *Planning, revising and editing are crucial elements in developing independent writers.*

» *The imagination is the muscle that makes the mechanics come to life.*

Chapter reflections

This chapter has explored the complexity of the writing process in terms of composition for effective written communication. It has emphasised that the mechanics of composition must work alongside imaginative exploration of understanding and ideas. Children must not only learn about grammar, punctuation and text cohesion, they must also understand how they come together to impact on the reader. If you refer back to 'what do good writers do?' at the beginning of this chapter, you will see that the first bullet point emphasises enjoyment. If your teaching is motivating and purposeful then the children will begin to understand, understanding will lead to success and success will lead to enjoyment and a desire to write. Through their writing, even the quietest child can find their voice.

Taking it further

Standards and Testing Agency (2014) *English Grammar, Punctuation and Spelling Test Framework (draft) 2016.* [online] Available at: www.gov.uk/government/publications (accessed 30 November 2014).

Waugh, D, Warner, C, and Waugh, R (2013) *Teaching Grammar, Punctuation and Spelling in Primary Schools*, London: Learning Matters.

References

Crystal, D (2009) *The Cambridge Encyclopedia of Language*. Cambridge: Cambridge University Press.

Department for Education (DfE) (2013) *The National Curriculum in England: Key Stages 1 and 2 Framework Document*. London: DfE.

Kung Fu punctuation: www.youtube.com/watch?v=VZHUtOMYOXw.

Medwell, J A, Wray, D, Moore, G E, and Griffiths, V (2014) *Primary English: Theory & Practice* (7th edn). London: Learning Matters.

11 Drama: a toolkit for practitioners

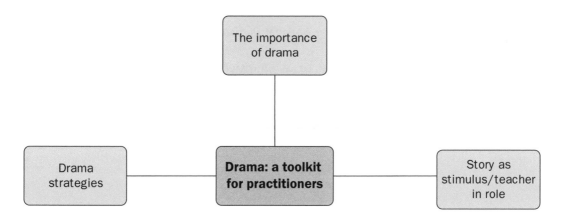

Teachers' Standards

TS3: Demonstrate good subject and curriculum knowledge

Trainees must:

*   have a secure knowledge of the relevant subject(s) and curriculum areas, foster and maintain pupils' interest in the subject, and address misunderstandings.

National curriculum links

Spoken language:

The national curriculum states that:

> All pupils should be enabled to participate in and gain knowledge, skills and understanding associated with the artistic practice of drama. Pupils should be able

to adopt, create and sustain a range of roles, responding appropriately to others in role. They should have opportunities to improvise, devise and script drama for one another and a range of audiences, as well as to rehearse, refine, share and respond thoughtfully to drama and theatre performances.

(DfE, 2013)

Introduction

Before you begin this chapter, it is important to differentiate between drama and theatre and define what is meant by these terms.

- **Drama** uses a range of forms of expression, including speech and gesture, to explore both real and imagined worlds. It is a shared experience that develops self-confidence, autonomy, social and interactive skills while improving the ability to communicate thoughts and knowledge.

- **Theatre** is taking drama techniques to a more polished outcome. Theatre is the art-form which results in the process becoming performance. It exists when the product of the drama is presented to an audience who respond and facilitate its development. For this reason, you also need to teach your pupils how to be an active audience, which requires good listening skills.

The two often merge and theatre will often result from the process that is drama. This chapter focuses on the process – the use of drama as a teaching and learning tool. It explores how drama techniques can develop as children mature and move from one primary phase (Key Stage 1) to the next (Key Stage 2).

This chapter does not tell you everything you need to know about drama but aims to motivate and inspire you to experiment with using drama in your teaching. The chapter provides you with some ideas but its key purpose is to hook you into drama so that you are motivated by its potential and inspired to use it both in English and across the curriculum.

Why do teachers avoid teaching drama? Perhaps they don't know how, or are scared of transferring the ownership of learning to the pupils and losing control, or they may be focused on pupils producing recorded work. If you feel like this, it is important to set your fears aside because drama is part of the national curriculum and is therefore an entitlement for every pupil. Teaching drama can be scary. It's about taking risks – but that is what outstanding trainees and teachers do.

The importance of drama

So why is drama so important? Essentially, it inspires pupils and engages them in their learning. It hooks them in. Even though they know it is all pretend, they still have an amazing capacity to go along with it. Finding hooks for learning is so important. If you can hook them in so that they want to learn that is half the battle won. You can then use the drama experience as a springboard for learning in other areas of the curriculum. If in Key Stage 1 pupils have interviewed the wolf in *The Three Little Pigs* story they will be able to write richer character descriptions. However, drama is not just a springboard for other learning. It is a subject in its own right. That said, drama can provide pupils with stimulating contexts for writing within a given purpose. Additionally, drama can enrich learning right across the curriculum. In Key Stage 1, pupils can learn more about the Great Fire of London by using role play to interview someone who witnessed the event. Equally, in Key Stage 2, the drama technique of Conscience Alley (see later in this chapter) can develop the necessary skills for persuasive writing.

Enrichment, motivation, engagement and the ability to inspire are all good solid reasons for doing drama. However, drama can also make a substantial contribution to pupils' social and emotional development. It can build confidence in dealing with social situations due to its emphasis on collaborative learning. It can also develop children's self-concepts and self-esteem. In Key Stage 1, this may be the exploration of our selves and learning to be a member of the class, while in Key Stage 2, it might develop a pupil's ability to deal with peer pressure within a unit of work on drugs education.

The role of drama across the curriculum

The examples in this chapter highlight the potential for using drama not just in English but right across the curriculum. The drama strategies can be taught within English but they can be applied in all subjects to add depth and enrichment to the learning experiences that you provide for pupils. The key point to note is that you should not be *teaching* the drama strategies in history, geography, science and so on. The strategies should be taught as part of a rich and varied English curriculum and they should then be used as a tool to promote learning across the curriculum.

Drama strategies

Teaching drama always involves an element of risk taking. Often, it may not be possible to predict exactly how your pupils will respond to the stimuli you offer them, and they may take the drama in a completely different direction from the one that you planned. This is not a bad thing. Great teachers take risks. They are also prepared to transfer ownership to their pupils by allowing them to lead the learning. They are able to take cues from the children and adapt the lesson as it evolves. Effective teachers of drama can respond in the moment to what their pupils are saying or doing and they realise it might not be possible to pre-determine the outcomes of the lesson.

In order to ensure that learning takes place you still need to maintain control of children's behaviour even if you transfer ownership of the learning to them. Understanding the key drama strategies will help you to loosely structure your lessons and provide a sense of coherence. Woolland (2010) emphasises the importance of getting children to develop the drama from the story, by going beyond the story rather than merely illustrating it. This is a critical point. You want pupils to actively engage in their learning and a fundamental part of this is to provide them with opportunities to make their own decisions and craft their own unique performances.

Paired improvisation

Paired improvisation is particularly useful when a decision needs to be made. Imagine that you are reading the story of *Jack and the Beanstalk* in Key Stage 1. Jack's mother decides that the family cow will have to be sold to provide money for food. They are starving and it is the only option. Pair the children so that one takes on the role of Jack and the other plays his mother. They discuss the situation. At first, Jack really doesn't want to sell the cow. In the paired improvisation they talk through the situation and listen and respond to the reasons given by each person. At the end of the drama they arrive at a decision. Throughout the improvisation there is no script to follow. The pair steer the conversation in the direction they want it to go. They then perform it to the rest of the class.

This strategy is superb for developing speaking and listening skills. It is also a good way of focusing on problem solving and it can be used across the curriculum.

Critical question

» *Consider the different ways that you might use this strategy across the curriculum. Try to give examples from at least two or three different subject areas.*

Tableaux

Children love this strategy. Essentially, it is the ability to create a frozen/still image. They usually find it hilarious at first, but you need to get them to be serious. They need to be able to hold the image on a given signal until you tell them to stop.

Imagine that you are teaching a topic on space. The pupils take on the role of townspeople carrying out their normal day-to-day activities. Some could be cleaning windows. Others could be sweeping the streets or serving customers in shops. You can allocate different duties to specific groups of pupils and they can even swap roles. Suddenly out of nowhere there appears an unidentified flying object. It lands on the road and out steps an alien. You need them to think about what their reactions might be at that particular time. What expressions would they have on their faces? Would they be frightened, surprised, scared or excited? Would they point at it or would they try to run away? Would they embrace the alien? Get them to think about what they might do when they first spot the UFO. Then get them to think about how they might react when the alien appears. On a given signal, ask them to hold a frozen or still image to reflect each situation. They might need to practise this several times. Take photographs of their frozen images (tell them not to laugh) and they can reflect on these at a later point.

Thought tracking

Imagine that your pupils are holding their frozen images in the above scenario. You are now going to 'thought-track' them. When you touch them on their shoulder they will say a word, caption or sentence to reflect one of the following:

• what they might be thinking at that specific point in time;

- how they might be feeling;

- what they can see;

- what they can hear.

Give them some thinking time first so that they can rehearse what they might say should you choose to touch their shoulder. It is useful to record their voices. You could then display the photographs of the still images and use speech bubbles to capture their thoughts and feelings at that particular point in time.

Critical questions

» *Consider how you might use tableaux and thought tracking across the curriculum.*

» *How would you model these strategies to pupils so that they understand what they are required to do?*

CASE STUDY

Example of thought tracking

A Year 2 class are studying the tale of *Cinderella*. The teacher wants them to explore the stock characters of 'goodie' and 'baddie' and has focused on Cinderella and the ugly sisters. The children have made a list of Cinderella's chores and the teacher chooses three pupils to take up the poses representing Cinderella undertaking these tasks: one scrubs the floor, one washes the dishes, while the third cleans the windows. She takes photographs to be used later. The teacher asks them to bring their picture to life and then freezes the scene. She then asks them to think of a phrase expressing Cinderella's thoughts/feelings as she works. One at a time, they unfreeze and speak their thoughts: *My fingers are so sore! Wash! Wash! Wash! I'm sick of this. These windows aren't even dirty.*

This is repeated several times as the teacher 'conducts' the pictures and voices.

She repeats the above exercise with the characters of the ugly sisters before bringing the characters together. Now the ugly sisters make demands on Cinderella, who responds respectfully:

US: *I want a pie for dinner!*

C: *Of course. What do you want in your pie?*

Again the teacher conducts the pictures and voices – asking some to repeat their phrase a number of times, resulting in a 'replay' technique.

The class are exploring the power relationship between the characters and now the teacher wants to take their learning a stage further. She introduces *'What I say/What I think'*. Three more children join the drama, each voicing one of Cinderella's thoughts. As the ugly sisters voice their demands, the audience can hear not only what Cinderella says to them, but also what she is really thinking, for example:

US: I want a pie for dinner!

C: (says) Of course. What do you want in your pie?

C: (thinks) I'd like to spit in your pie!

The teacher makes a recording of their voices and takes more photographs. These are used in a display of speech and thought bubbles.

In Key Stage 2, the above techniques can be extended into split screen or flashback/forward. Split screen allows you to explore two or more scenes or events at the same time. It develops the skills of contrasting and comparing and examines how characters or situations change over time. Similarly flashback/forward encourages pupils to go beyond what they know (the literal) and explore what they think and imagine (the inferential). Using the story of Goldilocks, you can explore her movements and motivations before she arrives at the cottage and after she flees. This technique can be used in either key stage and can result in the writing of prequels or sequels to well-known stories. In Year 2, one pupil I worked with once wrote about how Goldilocks ran to a nearby village carrying Baby Bear's bowl. He described her making her way to the village pub, going into the back room and opening a secret cupboard. Inside we find Robin Hood's bow, Red Riding Hood's cape and Cinderella's golden slipper – it turns out that Goldilocks was a serial thief.

Hot seating

This is a strategy through which pupils can ask questions or pose statements to a character who has been selected to sit in the hot seat. You might use this strategy to find out more about a character in a story you have read with your class. In the story of *Goldilocks and the Three Bears* you might decide to hot seat Baby Bear. You want to know:

*   how he feels about Goldilocks;
*   whether he would like to meet her again;
*   if he enjoys living in the forest.

You want your pupils to really get to know the character and this knowledge will take them beyond the story. They should then be able to use this information in their own creative writing, for example by writing a description of the forest.

This same story can be used in upper Key Stage 2 but now the questions and the characters become more analytical and explore social issues. A Year 6 class might ask questions such as: *What is Goldilocks doing out on her own, breaking into houses? Why hasn't she had any breakfast?* They might come to the conclusion that her family is dysfunctional and that outside agencies have become involved. They could then hot seat both Goldilocks and her social worker or set up a meeting between Goldilocks and Baby Bear to explore the relationship between victim and perpetrator. Drama is thus being used as a tool to explore the concept of restorative justice and can be extended to look beyond the fiction.

Hot seating can be used across the curriculum. In history, the pupils could hot seat Samuel Pepys or Florence Nightingale and this would work well after they have gained some knowledge of these famous people from their lessons. In science, they could hot seat famous scientists or they could hot seat an islander in geography. The possibilities are endless; once pupils become familiar with the strategy, it provides a rich opportunity to deepen their knowledge and extend their imaginations.

Hot seating does not have to stop at characters. To extend this technique in Key Stage 2, try exploring personification through the hot seating of inanimate objects, for example creating a back story for a suitcase.

Hot seating with very young children

Let's go back to the alien. The children are eager to find out as much as possible about the alien that has landed in your town. If you are hot seating with very young children you need to be sure that they understand what a question is. If they do not understand the concept of questions then they will not be able to hot seat the alien. So you need to spend time looking at questions. They need to know that questions begin with question words (*who, why, what, where, when, how,* etc) and that a question is not the same thing as a statement. You need to give them opportunities to sort questions from statements and they need to be taught about the function of a question mark. Then they need time to think of the questions that they might ask the alien. It is better to get them thinking in pairs first. They could jot down their questions (assuming they can write) or an adult could scribe them if you have the luxury of additional classroom support.

Then you need to decide who will be chosen to go in the hot seat to take on the role of the alien. Initially, you could decide to be the alien and so the pupils will direct the questions at you. You might even use face paints to colour your face to add a bit of excitement. If your pupils are not confident in asking questions you and another adult could model the process, or you could choose a confident child to go in the hot seat. Being in the hot seat can be challenging because you might not be able to predict what questions are going to be asked and you are literally improvising on the spot. However, practice makes perfect and the more you do this, the more confident the pupils will become.

Critical questions

» *Look through your planning and see if you can identify any opportunities for hot seating.*

» *How might you use hot seating at the beginning or end of a guided reading session?*

» *Make a list of specific questions you could ask your 'candidate'.*

» *What potential problems might there be with your scenario and how might you overcome these?*

Conscience alley

This strategy is particularly useful in Key Stage 2 but it can also be used in Key Stage 1. The class divides into two lines and they stand face to face with a gap (alley) between them. Each line takes on an opposing point of view. Choose a child to walk through the alley. The child visits each person in the line (usually zigzagging) and that person gives a perspective to represent the point of view that they are adopting. When they reach the end of the alley, the selected child has to decide which viewpoint to adopt, having listened to all the various perspectives. This method allows for the exploration of viewpoint and perspective, and can lead into writing discussion/persuasive texts in which there is the need to present two sides of an argument.

CASE STUDY

Key Stage 1 example: Little Red Riding Hood

Now consider how you might use this strategy in practice. In a Year 2 class the children are exploring traditional stories and have been reading the story of *Red Riding Hood*. Little Red Riding Hood cannot make her mind up about whether or not she should walk through the woods to visit her grandma. The teacher decides to do a Conscience Alley. One group try to persuade her to go. They give reasons such as:

*   *Grandma is lonely and needs company.*

*   *Grandma will get hungry and she needs food.*

*   *Grandma is ill and needs some help.*

The other group try to persuade Little Red to stay at home:

*   *You don't know what might be in the woods!*

*   *Grandma is ill and needs to rest.*

*   *The woods are dark. You might get lost.*

The pupils will need time to rehearse their responses before the drama takes place because you don't want them all saying the same things.

Key Stage 2 example: The Road Not Taken

In a Year 5/6 class the pupils are exploring classic poetry and are focused on 'The Road Not Taken' by Robert Frost. They are literally exploring the fork in the road that the protagonist must choose between and use Conscience Alley to give voice to their imaginations. They then take this a step further by introducing a scenario focusing on an issue being explored in PHSE, eg 'telling tales' and whether to lie for a friend – through Conscience Alley and the journey down each road, they explore the consequences.

Story as stimulus/teacher in role

A story or poem can be used as the basis for an enactment that may go far beyond the original. This can be particularly effective if the teacher acts in role, too. Let's look at a couple of case studies.

CASE STUDY

Key Stage 1 example: The Gruffalo

A teacher has chosen the story of *The Gruffalo* by Julia Donaldson and Axel Scheffler because of the suspense that it creates throughout the text. The children are asked to imagine that they are the Gruffalo. They live in the deep, dark wood and one morning they wake up and decide to go for a walk. After getting washed in the river, the Gruffalo walks further into the forest and stumbles across a house.

The teacher asks: *Who might live in the house?*

The children respond: *An old man!*

The teacher asks: *Do you think he is lonely?*

The children respond: *Yes, his family have left him and the animals in the forest are his only friends.*

The teacher asks: *Shall we talk to him?*

The children respond: *Yes, but what if he is angry that we have disturbed him?*

They decide to knock on the door. The teacher comes out in role as the old man.

Old man: *What do you want?*

Children: *We are Gruffaloes and we want to be friends with you.*

At this point, the children are hooked. They want this to continue. They want to learn more about the old man. You could now divide them into small groups and nominate one child per group to be the old man. The rest of the group will then ask the old man questions, and at the same time, the old man could think of questions to ask the Gruffaloes. They will need some thinking time in their groups to agree on the questions they want to ask. The Gruffaloes might want to know: *Why are you on your own? How do you get your food? What is it like living in the forest? Which animal is your best friend?* The old man might want to know: *What do Gruffaloes eat? What do you do with your sharp teeth? Why is your tongue black?*

The children are immersed in the drama. They want it to carry on. However, all of this has sprung from the teacher asking the question *who might live in the house?* The teacher has used the children's ideas to shape the lesson and the drama is only loosely connected with the original story of *The Gruffalo*. The teacher could not have planned all these aspects of the lesson because it was not possible to predict what ideas the children were going to suggest.

The teacher might then say to the class: *Shall we ask the old man if we can go inside his house to get warm?* And if they agree, the teacher can say: *I wonder what it is like in the old man's house. What might he own?*

The teacher could then give them time to think this through and provide opportunities to feed back their ideas. The teacher then stops the drama lesson and tells the children that they will find out more about the house next week. The teacher leaves them in suspense, looking forward to the next lesson.

Critical questions

» *Where would you take this role play?*

» *What questions might you introduce?*

CASE STUDY

Key Stage 2 example: The Angel of Nitshill Road

A Year 4 class are studying *The Angel of Nitshill Road* by Anne Fine, which the teacher has linked to their PHSE focus on bullying. They have explored the main characters who are being bullied by Barry Hunter and are now ready to take the drama further. The pupils, led by the teacher, imagine themselves in the playground – they are having fun playing games when 'Barry' (either played by another adult or represented by an inanimate object) arrives at the school gates and stands watching them. The teacher gathers them together and, in role as 'the Angel', encourages them to challenge his behaviour – they decide upon tactics. (At this point rules are introduced, eg there is to be no physical contact.)

Now in role as 'Barry', the teacher attempts to antagonise them – the pupils act out their agreed responses, eg all turn their backs on him. The action stops and the pupils ask 'Barry' how their actions make him feel.

Critical questions

» *How could you develop the 'Nitshill' scenario using this technique?*

» *Consider the different ways that you might use this strategy across the curriculum. Try to give examples from at least two or three different subject areas.*

It is common to ask pupils to write but without giving them any clear purpose or even audience. If you are going to motivate pupils to write you need to hook them in (this is often particularly true of boys). Setting up a scenario like the ones described above will give them a sense of purpose which is so important in writing. Think about the contexts that you set for writing and keep thinking of hooks to engage your pupils in learning. The more you do this, the more natural it will become. If they are hooked then it is likely that they will produce better quality work and you will have fewer issues to deal with in terms of discipline. Drama offers a rich tool for hooking pupils in and keeping them motivated.

Critical questions

» How can drama be used as a starting point to enrich children's writing?

» How can you collect evidence of pupils' learning in drama?

Critical points

» Drama strategies should be taught as part of an enriching and inspiring English curriculum.

» Drama strategies should be applied as a tool for learning across the curriculum.

» Drama potentially offers great hooks for learning which engage and inspire pupils.

» Drama should aim to take pupils beyond the texts they read to deepen their understanding of characters, settings and events.

Chapter reflections

This chapter has emphasised the importance of using drama both within English and across the curriculum. There are many reasons why you might want to avoid drama: you may feel you lack the required subject knowledge, you may be worried about losing control and you may be pressured into focusing on generating recorded outputs from pupils. However, drama can engage, motivate and inspire pupils. It can provide rich and exciting contexts and purposes for writing. It can enrich children's writing significantly. The ideas and vocabulary that they use in their drama can subsequently be applied to their writing, resulting in work of a much higher quality. However, drama is not just a tool for teaching writing or for learning across the curriculum. It is valid in its own right and it should be recognised and respected as such. Through drama you can motivate, inspire and engage pupils but you can also build their confidence in social interactions, speaking and presenting. It changes lives for the better and should therefore hold a significant place in the curriculum.

Taking it further

Baldwin, P (2008) *The Primary Drama Handbook: A Practical Guide for Teachers New to Drama and Teaching Assistants*. London: Sage.

This book offers practical examples on how to use drama in the primary school.

References

Department for Education (DfE) (2013) *The National Curriculum in England: Key Stages 1 and 2 Framework Document*. London: DfE.

Woolland, B (2010) *Teaching Primary Drama*. Essex: Pearson.

12 Reading for pleasure

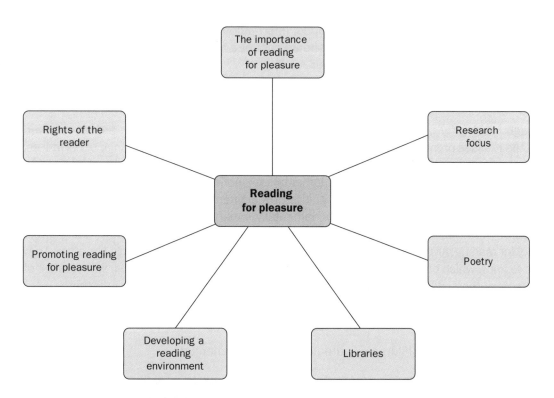

Teachers' Standards

TS3: Demonstrate good subject and curriculum knowledge

Trainees must:

- have a secure knowledge of the relevant subject(s) and curriculum areas, foster and maintain pupils' interest in the subject, and address misunderstandings.

National curriculum links

Reading: comprehension

The national curriculum states that:

> All pupils must be encouraged to read widely across both fiction and non-fiction to develop their knowledge of themselves and the world in which they live, to establish an appreciation and love of reading, and to gain knowledge across the curriculum. Reading widely and often increases pupils' vocabulary because they encounter words they would rarely hear or use in everyday speech. Reading also feeds pupils' imagination and opens up a treasure-house of wonder and joy for curious young minds.
>
> (DfE, 2013, p 14)

In Year 1, pupils are expected to hear, share and discuss a wide range of quality books to develop their vocabulary and their love of reading. In Year 2, pupils are expected to listen to and discuss a wide range of poems, stories, information books and plays, including whole books. Throughout Key Stage 2, pupils should continue to read fluently, independently and widely, demonstrating enthusiasm in their reading.

Introduction

Through reading for pleasure pupils can enter into imaginary worlds which are far removed from the realities of their everyday lives. Through listening to and reading a range of narratives, non-fiction and poetry, children's vocabulary will be extended and their imaginations will be developed. Additionally, reading is a fundamental tool for finding out about the world in which we live. Reading advances children's cognitive development and enables them to learn independently. As a trainee teacher, it is fundamentally important that you promote reading for pleasure. This chapter will discuss ways in which you can promote this through being a role model for reading. All teachers need to have a good understanding of children's literature. They need to know which books to introduce children to and they need to be familiar with a range of children's authors. Without this knowledge it is difficult to promote reading for pleasure.

The importance of reading for pleasure

Michael Rosen, former Children's Laureate, recently commented:

> We're talking about reading for pleasure, but what an odd thing to have to campaign for. It's kind of like saying 'Let's campaign for air, or for nice soup'. You read, you have a good time. That should be the end of it.
>
> (Michael Rosen, Hay Festival, 2014)

However, unfortunately reading for pleasure has become a luxury that many teachers cannot afford to invest time in. The pressures of a prescriptive national curriculum, school inspections, statutory assessments and league tables have resulted in a paradoxical situation in which schools and teachers find reading for pleasure difficult to justify.

Gaining pleasure from an activity makes that activity worthwhile and easy to justify in educational terms. However, children gain a great deal more than pleasure if they choose to read widely. Avid readers are able to increase their own knowledge rapidly as well as broadening their vocabularies and imaginations. Reading increases intelligence. Additionally, more practice in reading leads to concomitant improvements in writing abilities because children begin to internalise the essential skills of spelling, grammar and punctuation. As they start to read widely, children begin to absorb the conventions of expression and they are able to use these ideas in their own work.

The All-Party Parliamentary Group for Education stated that:

> *The active encouragement of reading for pleasure should be a core part of every child's curriculum entitlement because extensive reading and exposure to a wide range of texts make a huge contribution to students' educational achievement.*
>
> (All-Party Parliamentary Group on Education, 2011)

The new national curriculum (DfE, 2013) is now much less prescriptive than the former national curriculum. There is now more freedom for teachers to tailor the curriculum to meet the needs of their pupils and there is no prescribed model of teaching. Some teachers in some schools are still pinioned by the shackles of the National Literacy Strategy (DfEE, 1998), which introduced the literacy hour into primary schools. Lessons were compartmentalised and tightly structured and there was no time for children to hear or read whole texts or to write extensively. This led to practices such as teachers reading extracts of texts to pupils to fulfil specific objectives. An example of this approach would be a teacher reading an extract of a story setting to a class with a specific focus on identifying adjectives to describe nouns. The pupils would not hear the whole story but would focus on identifying the adjectives in the text. This approach reduces English to a technical exercise rather than promoting reading for pleasure. To gain real pleasure, children need to be transported into a story. They need to be engaged. They need to be completely absorbed in the events. They need to visualise themselves in the text. They need to be able to see the events unfolding in front of them as if they were there in the story. They need to share the feelings of suspense, excitement, joy, sadness and pain that the characters are experiencing. A good story absorbs the reader or listener through the power of evocative language. An extract from a text will not create this same sense of engagement because the reader or listener needs to share the full journey with the characters.

RESEARCH FOCUS

Key trends from academic research

The DfE published a report in 2012 entitled *Research Evidence on Reading for Pleasure* (DfE, 2012) which summarised key research findings. These included:

- Reading for pleasure enhances educational achievement and attainment as well as personal development (Clark and Rumbold, 2006).

- There is a positive relationship between frequency and enjoyment of reading and attainment (Clark 2011; Clark and Douglas 2011).

- Reading enjoyment has a greater impact on children's educational success than their family's socio-economic background (OECD, 2002).

- There is a positive link between positive dispositions towards reading and achieving highly on reading assessments (Twist et al, 2007).

- Regularly reading stories or novels outside of school is associated with higher achievement in reading assessments (Mullis et al, 2007; PISA, 2009).

- International evidence also supports these findings; US research reports that independent reading is the best predictor of reading achievement (Anderson et al, 1988).

- Reading for pleasure has a positive impact on children's social and emotional development (Clark and Rumbold, 2006).

- Other benefits to reading for pleasure include: text comprehension and knowledge of grammar, positive reading attitudes, pleasure in reading in later life, increased general knowledge (Clark and Rumbold, 2006).

(Research cited in DfE, 2012)

Critical questions

» *Why do you think reading for pleasure has a greater impact on attainment than social background?*

» *Think back to your own experiences as a child in primary school. Can you recall how it felt to listen to a really good story? Did you have story time?*

» *When was the last time you were absorbed in something that you read?*

» *What are the barriers which prevent you from reading for pleasure?*

» *How might these be overcome?*

» *How many children's books can you list from memory?*

» *How many children's authors can you name?*

» *How familiar are you with the work of these authors?*

» *What do you like to read?*

» *When and where do you like to read?*

» *Have you observed opportunities for children to read for pleasure during your placement experiences?*

Evidence also suggests that the majority of children reported that they do enjoy reading (Clark and Rumbold, 2006). In 2010, 22 per cent of children reported that they enjoyed reading very much; 27 per cent said they enjoyed it quite a lot; 39 per cent said they enjoyed it quite a bit, and 12 per cent reported that they did not enjoy reading at all (Clark 2011). Comparing against international evidence, children in England report that they read less frequently for pleasure outside of school than children in many other countries (Twist et al, 2007). Evidence consistently demonstrates that children enjoy reading less as they get older (Topping, 2010; Clark and Osborne, 2008; Clark and Douglas 2011). However, there is evidence to suggest that while the frequency with which young people read declines with age, the length for which they read when they read increases (Clark 2011). Several studies have indicated that boys enjoy reading less than girls and that children from working-class backgrounds read less for enjoyment than children from middle and upper social classes (Clark and Rumbold, 2006; Clark and Douglas 2011). Additionally, evidence has shown that children from Asian backgrounds have more positive attitudes to reading and read more frequently than children from white, mixed or black backgrounds (Clark and Douglas 2011). Research increasingly indicates that a growing number of children do not read for pleasure (Clark and Rumbold, 2006). Between 2000 and 2009, on average across OECD countries, the number of children who report reading for enjoyment daily dropped by five percentage points (OECD, 2010). This is supported by evidence from Mullis et al (2007) and Twist et al (2007), which found that attitudes towards reading had declined among children.

Critical questions

» *Why do you think that children from poorer socio-economic backgrounds read less for pleasure than children from more privileged social classes?*

» *How would you explain the differences in reading attitudes between the different ethnic groups?*

» *How would you explain the differences in reading attitudes between boys and girls?*

Boys and reading

Maloney (2000) found that boys like to read:

• humorous books;

• books which appeal to their sense of mischief;

• fantasy stories;

• science fiction;

• newspapers, comics, magazines, sports cards, instruction manuals;

• books which reflect their image of themselves – what they aspire to achieve.

Critical questions

» *How might views about gender preferences perpetuate gender stereotypes?*

» *What are the advantages and disadvantages of giving children gender-oriented texts?*

Ofsted findings

According to Ofsted:

> There has been considerable recent concern about an apparent decline in reading for pleasure. Evidence includes previous Ofsted reports, international surveys and the Evening Standard reading campaign... In too many schools there is no coherent policy on reading overall; schools put in place numerous programmes to support reading, especially for weak readers, but do not have an overall conception of what makes a good reader... Inspectors also noted the loss of once popular and effective strategies such as reading stories to younger children, listening to children read, and the sharing of complete novels with junior age pupils.
>
> (Ofsted, 2012, p 29)

Ofsted (2012) has highlighted that many primary school teachers have a very limited understanding of the world of children's literature. Although the report acknowledges that this is unsurprising due to the fact that many primary school teachers are not English subject-specialists, this does mean that teachers will find it difficult to suggest to children which texts they might wish to read. Additionally, limited knowledge of children's literature results in teachers being unable to challenge more able readers because they cannot suggest additional reading material for them (Ofsted, 2012). It is unlikely that English co-ordinators in primary schools will have studied English at degree level and this can have a detrimental impact on their understanding of the subject because they may not understand the techniques that writers use (Ofsted, 2012). Additionally, many primary school teachers are not able to identify writers from our rich literary heritage and many are not able to choose appropriate poetry for children to study. Inspectors found it worrying that the practice of reading complete novels to pupils in Key Stage 2 has declined, as has the practice of reading stories to younger children purely for enjoyment. These findings are supported by research demonstrating that primary teachers rely on a limited range of children's authors and can only name a few poets (Cremin et al, 2008a, 2008b).

These points raised by inspectors present a worrying picture. One way of addressing these issues is for schools to appoint a reading champion to promote reading (including reading for pleasure) across the curriculum. The reading champion would play a fundamental role in advising other teachers which texts to use across the full breadth of the curriculum. They would also develop a whole-school approach to reading for pleasure, being responsible for its implementation and monitoring its effectiveness.

Critical questions

» *How many poets can you name?*

» *How many children's poets specifically can you name?*

» *Is there a reading champion in your placement school?*

» *Is there a whole-school approach to reading for pleasure in your placement school?*

» *Is there a daily opportunity for young children to listen to stories in your placement school? If so, what time does this take place and what are the implications of this?*

According to the *Daily Telegraph*:

> *Children as young as 11 should be expected to read 50 books a year as part of a national drive to improve literacy standards... The vast majority of teenagers read one or two books as part of their GCSEs and [Mr Gove] said all schools should 'raise the bar' by requiring pupils to read a large number of books at the end of primary school and throughout secondary education.*
>
> (*Daily Telegraph*, 22 March 2011)

Critical questions

» *What is your response to this comment in the media?*

» *How can schools and teachers support children from households which are deprived of print to read for pleasure?*

» *How can schools support parents to read for pleasure?*

» *How can teachers exploit technological developments to encourage children to read for pleasure?*

» *How can schools ensure that the texts they purchase appeal to all pupils and reflect their interests?*

» *How can schools ensure that the texts they purchase challenge traditional stereotypes and prejudices?*

CASE STUDY

Promoting reading for pleasure

In one primary school which was recently visited, frames were displayed in every classroom. Inside each frame was a coloured copy of the front of a book cover. There was a caption which read 'This week, Miss X is reading...'. Every member of staff had their own frame, including the TAs and lunchtime supervisors who were attached to specific classes. A clear expectation permeated throughout the school that all staff would spend time reading for pleasure and there was also an expectation that the images in the frames would be changed on a regular basis each time the adult moved on to a different text.

Critical questions

» *In the above case study how important do you think whole-school leadership and management was in driving forward the agenda of adults reading for pleasure?*

Promoting reading for pleasure

Teachers as Readers

The United Kingdom Literacy Association (UKLA) published the results of a project entitled *Teachers as Readers: Building Communities of Readers* (Cremin et al, 2009). The aims of the project included:

- to improve teachers' knowledge and use of literature in order to increase children's motivation in reading;

- to develop teachers' knowledge of children's literature;

- to develop teachers' confidence in using children's literature.

The project arose from concerns that children in England read less independently and find reading less pleasurable than their peers in other countries (Twist et al, 2003, 2007; Mullis et al, 2007). The research took place in five local authorities and involved 40 teachers. The study found that disaffected readers became more engaged in reading and started to read more regularly and for pleasure when they were supported by motivated and knowledgeable teachers who had a good knowledge of children's literature. The teachers who participated in the research improved the provision of independent reading and the reading environments in their classrooms and the quality of *book talk* improved. The project suggested that there were very beneficial effects to developing reading teachers as role models. The development of reading teachers had a positive effect not only on children's reading dispositions and desire to read but also on children's overall achievements.

Crucially, the *Teachers as Readers* project distinguished between the pedagogy of reading for pleasure and reading instruction. Evidence suggested that reading for pleasure is oriented towards:

- *choosing to read;*

- *developing the will to want to read;*

- *developing engagement and response;*

- *developing lifelong readers;*

- *child direction;*

- *child ownership;*

- *achievement;*

- *the maximum entitlement – a reader for life.*

(Cremin et al, 2009)

In contrast, reading instruction was oriented towards:

- *learning to read;*

- *the skills of decoding and comprehension;*

- *system readers;*

- *teacher direction;*

- *teacher ownership;*

- *attainment;*

- *the minimum entitlement – a 'level 4';*

- *the standards agenda.*

(Cremin et al, 2009)

Reading for pleasure is distinct from reading instruction because it places more focus on children taking ownership of their learning and making choices about what they want to read. It can be created by creating reading communities that are characterised by reciprocity and interaction. Reciprocal reading communities share the following characteristics:

- *they acknowledge diverse reader identities;*

- *they are social places that encourage choice and child ownership of their own reading for pleasure;*

- *teachers and children demonstrate extensive knowledge of children's literature;*

- *readers have agency and independence;*

- *there is a shared concept of what it means to be a twenty-first-century reader.*

(Cremin et al, 2009)

Critical questions

» *What does it mean to be a twenty-first-century reader? Discuss this with your colleagues.*

» *Why is the maximum entitlement of being a reader for life so important?*

The Rooted in Reading project

The *Rooted in Reading* project which was implemented in Lincolnshire introduced the use of reading passports. These are designed to encourage pupils to read a range of text types and pupils are rewarded each time they finish reading a book. The aim is that children are rewarded through the use of extrinsic rewards, including stamps and certificates for reading for pleasure. The research found that the use of the passports had a positive impact in schools in deprived areas, suggesting that the passports might help to narrow the achievement gap in reading between children in deprived areas and those in more affluent areas. Children's attainment increased in schools which made extensive use of the passports and their stamina also increased. More information on the project can be found at www.rooted-inreading.co.uk/.

CASE STUDY

ERIC

A primary school adopted a whole-school approach to reading for pleasure known as ERIC (**E**veryone **R**eading **i**n **C**lass). At a specific time each day (in this case it was immediately after lunch) all classes had a 20-minute period of reading for pleasure. Children were free to select their own texts from a pre-determined range and older children were encouraged to select a longer text and keep it for several days until they had finished reading it. This encouraged them to develop stamina in reading. The role of the adults was critical during this period of time. They used it as an opportunity to model reading for pleasure by sitting down with a book of their own choice and reading it alongside the children.

Critical questions

In the above case study:

» *How important is it that the children read in silence? Is there value in encouraging them to share books collaboratively?*

» *What could you do during this time to support readers at the very early stages of development, for example, those who are not yet reading?*

» *Are there any benefits in pairing children up during these lessons, for example encouraging a more able reader to support a less able reader? Are there any limitations of this approach?*

World Book Day

World Book Day is a fantastic opportunity to promote reading for pleasure. Schools usually encourage their pupils to come to school dressed as their favourite book character and teachers are usually expected to do the same. The day provides a context for hooking children into literature. You will need to consider how you can plan the curriculum around children's literature. The day could involve a variety of activities. These could include:

• oral story-telling;

• listening to stories read aloud by the teacher;

• opportunities for pupils to share books with each other;

• opportunities for pupils to write stories;

• making books;

• mathematical problems linked to stories.

You might want to base all the activities for the day upon a specific text. In this instance, you will need to identify ways in which the text could be used as a context for learning in other areas of the curriculum, including science and design and technology. Stories can often be great contexts for setting problems in these subjects. Further information about World Book Day can be found on the following site: www.worldbookday.com/.

Author days

One way of hooking pupils into reading is to invite an author, illustrator, poet or story-teller into the classroom to work alongside the pupils. The aim of the visit is to hook children into reading. You could invite a local poet or a famous author into the classroom to talk to the children about the work they do and why they choose to do it. The author could work with the children in a range of ways. Further information on arranging author days can be found on the following sites:

» *www.authorsalouduk.co.uk/*

» *www.booktrust.org.uk/programmes/arranging-an-author-visit/*

» *www.scatteredauthors.org/index.htm*

Rights of the reader

The National Union of Teachers has promoted reading for pleasure through a publication entitled *Reading 4 Pleasure.* This is an extremely useful document which includes research findings and practical classroom strategies for developing reading for pleasure in classrooms. The document lists ten inviolable readers' rights.

1. The right not to read;

2. The right to skip pages;

3. The right not to finish a book;

4. The right not to reread;

5. The right to read anything;

6. The right to 'bovarysme' (to read for the instant satisfaction of our feelings);

7. The right to read anywhere;

8. The right to browse;

9. The right to read out loud;

10. The right to remain silent (not to have to comment on what has been read).

These rights could be displayed in the classroom and in reading areas and school libraries.

Critical questions

» *Do you agree with these rights?*

» *Do you want to add to them or delete any of them?*

Developing a reading environment

Developing a suitable classroom environment to promote reading for pleasure is critical to fostering good attitudes towards reading. You should aim to create attractive, stimulating reading areas in your classrooms that include a range of quality fiction, non-fiction and poetry texts. These should be displayed with outward-facing covers so that children are immediately attracted to the texts. You might want to consider including some cushions or soft seating in your reading area to aid comfort. Think carefully about the displays you might create in this area. You could include posters about significant children's authors or colour copies of book covers. A reading tree is a really easy way of enabling children to make recommendations about specific texts. Using leaf-shaped paper, they could write their recommendations for specific texts and display these on a tree to encourage other children to read those texts.

You might wish to display three or four books on a table which you recommend the children read. You could leave these books out for the children to access independently and you could ask them later to say what they thought about them. Encourage your pupils to give honest, open views about the texts they read. Different types of texts appeal to different people and children need to be taught from a very early stage of development that people have individual preferences in relation to reading. Make sure that you plan into your daily timetable opportunities for children to read in this area. It should not just be an area that children access when they have finished a piece of work because this devalues reading. You need to value reading as an important activity which promotes enjoyment and academic attainment. This needs to be central to your values and beliefs as a teacher.

Ensure that children have specific periods of time each day when they read for pleasure and allow them to make their own choices in terms of the books they want to read. You might want to think about including specific texts in the reading area that relate to a class theme or topic. Involve the children in planning the area. Ask them what types of texts they would like to see there and consult with them regularly so that they are included in making key decisions about their learning. Change the texts regularly and include texts that cater for a range of abilities. Make sure that you have included texts which reflect social and cultural diversity and texts which challenge traditional stereotypes. Some children's texts which have stood the test of time (such as *The Tiger Who Came to Tea*) can still be enjoyed, but use this as an opportunity to challenge the stereotypes which are evident in these books.

Encourage your pupils to keep a reading journal so that they have an opportunity to review the books they have read. You could create a *book review space* on a class blog on your school website to provide children with an opportunity to post comments about books they have read and to share these with others.

Libraries

Promote the use of the local library to your pupils and even consider arranging a visit to the library so that they become familiar with it. Encourage parents to take their children to the library and include notices about it in your reading area. Many primary schools now have very sophisticated school libraries which have electronic booking systems and self-service returns. This encourages children to take responsibility for the books they borrow. School libraries are most effective when classes have a dedicated time each week to visit the library. Schools can involve designated pupils to take responsibility for the library in order to make sure that it is being respected. These pupils could be designated as *reading champions* and they could play a critical role in promoting reading for pleasure to their peers. The library should be well organised and well stocked with a range of quality texts, including texts for adults so that teachers and TAs can model promoting reading for pleasure.

Critical questions

»   *How important are libraries in the community?*

»   *How important is the school library?*

»   *How important is it that children access texts in their printed form?*

»   *How can schools exploit developments in technology to enhance the resources in their libraries?*

Poetry

If we are serious about literacy, then poetry should be seen as one of the most important parts of the process. When children hear it, they are hearing feelings, thoughts and ideas coming at them with, through and as a result of how the language can sound. When they read it, they are helped by the echoing effects of rhyme, rhythm and musical sounds. When they write it, they get a chance to play with language, and discover that they can control language instead of being controlled by it. And when they perform and publish their poems they get a chance to be real authors and discover what 'audience' means and how it affects what we write.

All this is why it's vital that teachers of all kinds, but especially newcomers to the profession, get access to a range of poets and poetry so that they can make their classrooms full of the richness of poetic thought and language.

Michael Rosen in *Learning about children's books and poetry: tips and resources for trainee teachers*, www.booktrust.org.uk

The national curriculum states that schools must introduce children to poetry and there is an explicit focus on children learning poetry by heart. However, many trainee teachers and teachers lack confidence in teaching poetry and this is partly because their own subject knowledge is under-developed. Reading areas should include a range of different types of age-appropriate poems which include both rhyming and non-rhyming poems, shape poems, humorous poems, riddles, haiku, concrete poetry, alliterative poems, onomatopoeia poetry, cinquain. This is not an exhaustive list and the range of poetry types can be extended as children's confidence increases. It is essential that you model your passion for poetry as a teacher. This needs to come through in the way you read poetry to children. You need to use your voice effectively, ensuring that you read with expression. You need to spend time discussing the structure of the poem, the vocabulary and phrases that poets have used in their poems and the impact they are trying to make on the reader (reading as a writer).

Children need opportunities to hear you reading and performing poetry as well as opportunities to read poems in pairs, groups, as a class or individually. Additionally, children need to be introduced to different poets and their styles. Humorous poems will appeal to children's sense of fun and this is a good way into poetry. *Revolting Rhymes* by Roald Dahl appeals to children's sense of humour and has stood the test of time. You need to get children engaged and obsessed about reading poetry and learning about poets in the same way that you need to get them obsessed about reading stories and non-fiction texts.

When you discuss poems with children, focus on how the poet has used rhyme, alliteration, metaphor, simile, repetition, vocabulary and structure or presentation to create an effect on the reader. Ask children to close their eyes as you read a poem aloud to them and to create a visual representation in their minds. What picture do they have in their mind as they listen to the poem? Ask them to articulate this to their response partner or to the whole class. Ask them to draw the image they have created in their minds after they have listened to a poem. Focus their attention on how the poet may have played around with language to invent new words. Then give children the opportunity to play with language and invent their own words. Playing with language is one way in which children can take control of language rather than being controlled by it and Michael Rosen highlights the importance of this in the above quote. Consider developing children's familiarity with one poem and encourage them to learn it by heart, perform it and evaluate it. Give them opportunities to adapt a familiar poem by changing words or lines before you ask them to create poems completely from scratch. Ask them to write simple reviews of poems and to make recommendations to each other by filling in reviews in the reading area. Display poems in the classroom and outside in the playground so that children encounter poetry as they do other things.

Critical points

» *Reading for pleasure enhances academic attainment and life chances.*

» *Reading for pleasure promotes reading for life.*

» *Senior leadership teams need to engender a whole-school culture of promoting and valuing reading for pleasure.*

» *Teachers who champion reading will shape the development of positive attitudes towards reading among their pupils.*

» *You have a responsibility to value and promote reading for pleasure.*

» *You have a responsibility to be knowledgeable about children's literature.*

» *You have a responsibility to be familiar with contemporary children's fiction.*

» *Reading is more than decoding and comprehension – reading is about enjoyment and having fun.*

Chapter reflections

This chapter has introduced you to some of the significant research on reading for pleasure. It has also introduced you to some pedagogical ideas which will help you to promote reading for pleasure in school. On your next placement you should make a determined effort to promote a reading for pleasure agenda in your classroom. You cannot inspire children to read for pleasure if you do not enjoy reading. If you do not read regularly, set yourself a target of reading one book each month for just ten minutes each day. Get into the habit of reading on the bus or on the train or as you sit in the garden. Choose what you want to read but, above all, gain pleasure from it. A reading teacher will excite, engage and motivate children. You cannot hope to get children obsessed about reading if you are not a reader.

Taking it further

www.nfer.ac.uk/publications/PSTT01/PSTT01ExecutiveSummary.pdf

www.teachers.org.uk/node/12394

www.teachers.org.uk/files/active/1/Reading-4-Pleasure-7225.pdf

www.poetrysociety.org.uk

www.performapoem.lgfl.org.uk

www.nationalpoetryday.co.uk

www.clpe.co.uk

www.children'spoetrybookshelf.co.uk

www.nawe.co.uk

www.literacytrust.org.uk

www.sla.org.uk

www.readingagency.org.uk

www.ukla.org

www.writeaway.org.uk

www.booktrust.org.uk

www.poetryfriendlyclassroom.org.uk

www.everybodywrites.org.uk

Recommended poetry books

1. *Michael Rosen's A to Z* by Michael Rosen

2. *New and Collected Poems for Children* by Carol Ann Duffy

3. *Revolting Rhymes* by Roald Dahl

4. *Collected Poems* by Allan Ahlberg

5. *J is for Jamaica* by Benjamin Zephaniah

6. *Cloud Bursting* by Malorie Blackman

7. *Sensational! Poems Inspired by the Five Senses* by Roger McGough (ed)

8. *Collected Poems for Children* by Ted Hughes

9. *Red Cherry Red* by Jackie Kay

10. *Heartbeat* by Sharon Creech

Recommended by www.booktrustchildrensbooks.org.uk

References

All-Party Parliamentary Group for Education (2011) *Report of the Inquiry into Overcoming Barriers to Literacy.* [online] Available at: www.educationengland.org.uk/documents/pdfs/2011-appge-literacy-report.pdf (accessed 14 October 2014).

Anderson, R C, Wilson, P T, and Fielding, L G (1988) Growth in Reading and How Children Spend Their Time outside of School. *Reading Research Quarterly*, 23(3): 285–303 (http://eric.ed.gov/?id=EJ373263, accessed 30 November 2014).

Clark, C (2011) *Setting the Baseline: The National Literacy Trust's first annual survey into reading – 2010.* London: National Literacy Trust.

Clark, C, and Douglas, J (2011) *Young People's Reading and Writing: An in-depth study focusing on enjoyment, behaviour, attitudes and attainment,* London: National Literacy Trust.

Clark, C, and Osborne, S (2008) *How Does Age Relate to Pupils' Perceptions of Themselves as Readers?* London: National Literacy Trust.

Clark, C, and Rumbold, K (2006) *Reading for Pleasure a research overview.* London: National Literacy Trust.

Cremin, T, Bearne, E, Goodwin, P, and Mottram, M (2008a) Primary teachers as readers. *English in Education*, 42 (1): 1–16.

Cremin, T, Mottram, M, Bearne, E, and Goodwin, P (2008b) Exploring teachers' knowledge of children's literature. *Cambridge Journal of Education*, 38 (4): 449–64.

Cremin, T, Mottram, M, Collins, F, Powell, S, and Safford, K (2009) *Teachers as Readers: Building Communities of Readers 2007–08 Executive Summary.* London: UK Literacy Association.

Department for Education (DfE) (2012) *Research Evidence on Reading for Pleasure.* London: DfE.

Department for Education (DfE) (2013) *The National Curriculum in England: Key Stages 1 and 2 Framework Document.* London: DfE.

Department for Education and Employment (DfEE) (1998) *The National Literacy Strategy: Framework for Teaching.* London: DfEE.

Maloney, J (2000) *Boys and Books: Building a Culture of Reading Around Our Boys.* Springfield, MO: ABC Books.

Mullis, I V S, Martin, M O, Kennedy, A M, and Foy, P (2007) Students' Reading Attitudes, Self-Concept, and Out-of-School Activities, in *IEA's Progress in International Reading Literacy Study in Primary School in 40 Countries.* Boston College: TIMSS & PIRLS, Ch 4, pp 139–55. [online] Available at: http://timss.bc.edu/PDF/P06_IR_Ch4.pdf (accessed 6 October 2014).

OECD (2002) *Reading For Change Performance And Engagement Across Countries – Results From PISA 2000*. Paris: OECD.

Office for Standards in Education (2012) *Moving English Forward: Action to Raise Standards in English*. London: Ofsted.

PISA (2009) [online] Available at: www.oecd.org/pisa/keyfindings/pisa2009keyfindings.htm (accessed 6 October 2014).

Topping, K J (2010) *What Kids Are Reading: The Book-Reading Habits of Students in British Schools, 2010*. London: Renaissance Learning UK.

Twist, L, Schagen, I, and Hodgson, C (2003) *Readers and Reading: The National Report for England*, PIRLS, Slough: NfER.

Twist, L, Schagan, I and Hodgson, C (2007) *Progress in International Reading Literacy Study (PIRLS): Reader and Reading National Report for England 2006*. London: NFER and DCSF.

Conclusion

We want to emphasise two key points that we believe are vital. We have deliberately included them in this conclusion because if you take nothing else from this book, we want you to remember these points.

1. Do not stifle children's reading by tightly restricting access to texts. Let them choose which books they want to read. Allow them to read things they are interested in and give them opportunities to voice their opinions about which texts to include in the classroom. Restricting their choices and only allowing them to read material selected by a teacher will not encourage them to read for pleasure and may lead to them disengaging from reading.

2. Give children time to develop and shape their own ideas for their writing. Celebrate their creative ideas and help them to develop them further. Do not be overly prescriptive about what they write. Allow them to make choices about what they write and give them some ownership about how they wish to present their work. In the early stages of writing, accept and celebrate children's invented spellings and celebrate their emergent writing.

We have emphasised throughout this book the importance of hooking children into English. Pupils need stimulating contexts to develop as speakers, listeners, readers and writers. You need to carefully engineer these contexts so that learning becomes relevant and purposeful. Pupils need to speak, read and write for a range of purposes and audiences, and they need opportunities to use the skills of speaking, listening, reading and writing across the full breadth of the primary curriculum. Pupils also need opportunities to read for information and for pleasure. In addition, pupils need to be provided with opportunities to speak and write for pleasure.

Your role as teachers and future teachers is to get children buzzing about English. Decontextualised grammar, spelling and punctuation exercises serve little purpose. On the other hand, if you teach these elements through the medium of texts, children will begin to understand how writers have made specific choices in order to create a greater impact on the reader. It is then that grammar and punctuation become meaningful because pupils can place it in the contexts of the texts that they are reading. When the skills of English are taught within the context of texts, pupils will start to use grammar and punctuation for effect in their own writing in the same way that authors do.

Children need to see themselves as authors and poets. They need to be introduced throughout their primary education to a rich tapestry of stories, poems and non-fiction texts. It is your role to empower them and help them to believe in their abilities to be authors. Creating a positive climate for learning in the classroom where pupils' attempts at speaking, reading and writing are valued and celebrated is one way of motivating young learners. Being a role model yourself is another way of inspiring them. You cannot expect pupils to be readers or authors if you do not model being a reader or a writer. Sharing examples of your own writing and the texts you are reading with your pupils will help them to understand that the skills of English are important for both adults and children. Having a broad knowledge of children's literature is essential in order for you to be able to challenge children further in reading and ignite children's passion for reading.

You need to be brave in your approaches to teaching. There is no 'correct' model of how to teach an English lesson. Children tend to disengage with predictable lesson structures and they enjoy lessons that are varied and use a range of approaches. You need to focus on hooking them into learning, getting them engaged in the learning and getting them obsessed about speaking, listening, reading and writing. Reducing teacher talk, getting pupils on task and giving them sufficient time to practise their skills are critical aspects of effective pedagogy, not just in English, but in all aspects of the curriculum.

Glossary

Some definitions are taken directly from the national curriculum (DfE, 2013).

Adjacent consonant	Adjacent consonants are next to each other either at the beginning or end of words, eg f l a g, c r i s p. Each individual consonant represents a separate sound (phoneme).
Adverb	Adverbs modify a verb, an adjective, another adverb or even a whole clause. *James quickly started shouting loudly.* [Adverbs modifying the verbs *started* and *shouting*]
Alphabetic code	In English the sounds of speech are represented by letters and this is known as the alphabetic code.
Blending	This is the process in which sounds (phonemes) are pronounced in sequence within a word and put together to read the target word.
Clause	A clause is a special type of phrase whose head is a verb. Clauses can sometimes be complete sentences. Clauses may be main or subordinate.
Consonant digraph	A consonant digraph is two consonants next to each other which represent one sound (phoneme), eg shop or chip.
Decoding	Decoding is the process of translating the symbols (graphemes) of a word into a spoken word. When we read a word by sounding it out we are decoding the word.
Digraph	This is a written representation of a phoneme using two letters. • Vowel digraphs: these represent vowel *sounds* and can be made up purely of vowels (ee/ea/oa/ue/ai) or can include consonants (e.g. say) • Consonant digraphs: see above.

Encoding	When a spoken word is translated into written symbols this is known as encoding or segmenting. We use this process for spelling.
Exception word	These are words that include unusual grapheme–phoneme correspondences. For example, in the word s*ai*d the grapheme in the middle of the word represents the sound /e/.
Grapheme	A letter, or combination of letters, that corresponds to a single *phoneme* within a word. It is the written representation of a phoneme.
Guided reading	Reading which takes place within a small group using a text which has been specifically chosen to meet the needs of that group of pupils.
Inference	The ability to infer refers to the ability to piece together known information to make a deduction.
Linguistic comprehension	Linguistic comprehension refers to the ability to understand spoken vocabulary.
Noun	Nouns are sometimes called 'naming words' because they name people, places and things; this is often true, but it doesn't help to distinguish nouns from other word classes. For example, prepositions can name places and verbs can name 'things' such as actions. Nouns may be classified as **common** (eg *boy*, *day*) or **proper** (eg *Ivan*, *Wednesday*), and also as **countable** (eg *thing*, *boy*) or **non-countable** (eg *stuff*, *money*). These classes can be recognised by the determiners they combine with.
Noun phrase	A noun phrase is a phrase with a noun as its head, eg *some foxes*, *foxes with bushy tails*. Some grammarians recognise one-word phrases, so that *foxes are multiplying* would contain the noun *foxes* acting as the head of the noun phrase *foxes*.
Onset	The onset refers the consonants that come before the vowel for example in *string* the onset is 'str'.
Oral rehearsal	This refers to the process of articulating ideas before writing them down.
Phoneme	A phoneme is the smallest unit of sound that signals a distinct, contrasting meaning. There are around 44 phonemes in English; the exact number depends on regional accent. A single phoneme may be represented in writing by one, two, three or four letters constituting a single grapheme.
Phonemic awareness	Phonemic awareness refers to the ability to perceive and manipulate the phonemes in spoken words (Johnston and Watson, 2007). A child with good phonemic awareness can identify the three phonemes in *boat*, ie /b/oa/t/.

Phonological awareness	Phonological awareness refers to the ability to perceive and manipulate syllables, onsets and rimes within words (Johnston and Watson, 2007).
Prefix	A prefix is added at the beginning of a word in order to turn it into another word.
Pronoun	A pronoun is a word which is substituted to replace a noun, eg *he, she, them*.
Reading as a writer	Reading as a writer is characterised by the ability to read a piece of text while identifying specific ways in which the writer has used vocabulary, grammar and punctuation to create an impact on the reader.
Register	Classroom lessons, football commentaries and novels use different registers of the same language, recognised by differences of vocabulary and grammar. Registers are varieties of language which are each tied to a range of uses, in contrast with dialects, which are tied to groups of users.
Rime	The rime is the vowel and the rest of the syllable, eg in *sting* the rime is 'ing'.
Segmenting	Segmenting is the ability to split a spoken word into phonemes and to represent these as graphemes to spell the word. See also 'encoding'.
Semantic knowledge	This refers to the ability to get meaning from a sentence.
Shared reading	Shared reading is the sharing of a text usually with a class. The text is read with some participation from the audience.
Split vowel digraph	This is a vowel digraph split by a consonant. For example, in *name* the vowel digraph a-e is split with the consonant 'm'.
Standard English	Standard English can be recognised by the use of a very small range of forms such as *those books, I did it* and *I wasn't doing anything* (rather than their non-standard equivalents); it is not limited to any particular accent. It is the variety of English which is used, with only minor variations, as a major world language. Some people use standard English all the time, in all situations from the most casual to the most formal, so it covers most registers. The aim of the national curriculum is that everyone should be able to use standard English as needed in writing and in relatively formal speaking.
Subordinate clause	A clause which is subordinate to some other part of the same sentence is a subordinate clause; for example, in *The apple that I ate was sour*, the clause *that I ate* is subordinate to *apple* (which it modifies). Subordinate clauses contrast with co-ordinate clauses as in *It was sour but looked very tasty*. (Contrast: main clause). However, clauses that are directly quoted as direct speech are not subordinate clauses.

Suffix	A suffix is an ending, used at the end of one word to turn it into another word. Unlike root words, suffixes cannot ususaly stand on their own as a complete word.
Syllable	A syllable sounds like a beat in a word. Syllables consist of at least one vowel, and possibly one or more consonants.
Syntactic knowledge	Knowledge of syntax refers to the ability to understand the rules of sentence structure.
Synthetic phonics	Synthetic phonics refers to the process of separating words into phonemes and then blending the phonemes together in sequence to read the word. Words are broken down into the smallest meaningful units of sound within a word rather than into larger units such as rimes.
Tenses	In English, tense gives an indication of time. Words can be written in the present, continuous, past and future tense. In contrast, languages like French, Spanish and Italian have three or more distinct tense forms, including a future tense. In English, the simple tenses (present and past) may be combined with the perfect and progressive.
Trigraph	A type of grapheme where three letters represent one phoneme
Verb	Verbs are sometimes called 'doing words' because many verbs name an action that someone does; while this can be a way of recognising verbs, it doesn't distinguish verbs from nouns (which can also name actions). Moreover, many verbs name states or feelings rather than actions. Verbs can be classified in various ways: for example, as auxiliary, or modal; as transitive or intransitive; and as states or events.
Word recognition	Word recognition is the ability to translate graphemes on a page into their constituent phonemes then to blend these together to read words. It also refers to the skill of identifying whole words from visual memory.
Writing as a reader	Writing as a reader refers to composing text while being consciously aware of how to use vocabulary, grammar and punctuation to create an impact on the reader.

Index